DANCING WITH DATA TO IMPROVE LEARNING

Dave Sever

ScarecrowEducation
Lanham, Maryland • Toronto • Oxford
2004

Published in the United States of America
by ScarecrowEducation
An imprint of The Rowman & Littlefield Publishing Group, Inc.
4501 Forbes Boulevard, Suite 200, Lanham, Maryland 20706
www.scarecroweducation.com

PO Box 317
Oxford
OX2 9RU, UK

British Library Cataloguing in Publication Information Available

Library of Congress Cataloging-in-Publication Data

Sever, Dave, 1951–
    Dancing with data to improve learning / Dave Sever.
        p. cm.
    Includes bibliographical references.
    ISBN 1-57886-171-3 (pbk. : alk. paper)
    1. Educational tests and measurements—United States—Evaluation. 2.
Academic achievement—United States—Evaluation. 3. School improvement
programs—United States. I. Title.
LB3051.S395 2004
379.1'58—dc22

                                                2004011639

∞™ The paper used in this publication meets the minimum requirements of
American National Standard for Information Sciences—Permanence of Paper
for Printed Library Materials, ANSI/NISO Z39.48-1992.
Manufactured in the United States of America.

For her inspiration, support, encouragement, and patience throughout this dance, I dedicate this book to my loving wife and partner, Cheryl.

CONTENTS

Introduction		vii
1	Choose to Dance, But ...	1
2	Don't Fox Trot in a Disco	9
3	Don't Trip over Your Own Feet	35
4	Don't Stop When You're Tired—Just Change Your Routine	43
5	Don't Sidestep the Issues	57
6	Try Some Fancy Footwork	63
Glossary		67
Bibliography		71
About the Author		77

INTRODUCTION

When I began teaching in the 1970s, aside from conventional standardized tests, there were few means for holding teachers and schools accountable for what they were teaching. While we glanced at the data that traditional standardized tests provided, little emphasis was placed on this information. As we moved into the 1980s, we began to experience fallout from such highly publicized documents as *Why Johnny Can't Read* and the 1983 report *A Nation at Risk*. Policymakers and public officials began to doubt our public school system. Concerns and public outcries resulted in the launching of bandwagons and panaceas for "fixing" the system. The plight of high-stakes standardized testing had begun!

Generally, standardized tests and the data they provide can and should be of great value to us. However, data can be and are often grossly misused. Much of the misuse stems from a lack of understanding by those who should (and some who even profess to) understand them.

Such lack of understanding and misunderstanding can have quite negative effects. The advent of the "No Child Left Behind" legislation has caused frustration, confusion, and often a division among educators and policymakers in regard to what data to use and how to use them.

This in turn raises questions among parents as to how to actually determine which schools provide the "best" education. Perhaps the ultimate in confusion became reality in August 2002 when it was reported in *USA Today* (Thomas & DeBarros, 2002) that "19 of USA's 'finest' schools are 'failing.'" The report read:

> At least 19 schools dubbed the nation's finest by the federal government over the past five years are also on this year's state lists of failing schools. . . .
>
> The overlap underscores just how elusive the definition of "school excellence" has become and questions the validity of the nation's most prestigious recognition program.
>
> Since 1982 the U.S. Department of Education has honored nearly 4,000 Blue Ribbon schools, based on a 50-page application and a site visit. Winning gives a school bragging rights and can drive up home prices.
>
> In January, President Bush signed his education reform bill requiring states to compile a list of all schools that don't make adequate progress in academics for two years in a row. There are 8,652 such "failing" schools.
>
> *USA Today* compared 1,154 Blue Ribbon schools with the failing schools in the 10 states with the largest number. . . .
>
> Of the states studied, *USA Today* found half had at least one Blue Ribbon winner among schools that failed to meet state standards. At least seven were simultaneously the nation's "best" and "worst" in the 2000–2001 school year; three won the exemplary title in May, just one month before the federal deadline to report failing schools.
>
> "No way should those two intersect," says Tom Loveless, director of the Brown Center on Education Policy at the Brookings Institution. He calls the message "convoluted. . . . What's the public supposed to believe?" Finding so many overlaps in just 10 states "lowballs the real problem" nationwide, he says. "It's just the tip of the iceberg."
>
> Federal education officials say it's not fair to compare the two programs because they measure different kinds of school progress. Even so, once the unexpected contradiction became apparent, U.S. Secretary of Education Rod Paige announced last week new criteria for the Blue Ribbon program. Cuts will be made to its $1.1 million budget.
>
> "Failing" schools include about one-fifth of the nation's Title I-funded schools—those that get federal money to teach disadvantaged students. Even if a school shows improved test scores it may be considered failing if progress isn't also seen in subgroups such as low-income, special education, limited English and minorities. (p. 1)

The misfortune of this scenario is that our students and teachers are caught in the precarious middle. Misinterpretation and misuse of data often devastate teachers and place undue pressure on their students. The result is teachers who "teach the test" rather than what may be best for their students. Furthermore, ever changing targets and expectations cause stress, uncertainty, and consternation for teachers and administrators who strive to follow the rules, play the game, and try to do what is best for our youngsters.

The issue of "changing targets" is outlined in the example illustrated above. Too many people with too many criteria for change add to the confusion. Perhaps all are well intentioned. Maybe some are not. It is quite noble that we want no child to be left behind. Certainly few can argue with that notion.

I heard a speaker a few months ago who shared a conversation he had had with a public official around the newly adopted legislation, "No Child Left Behind." The public official remarked about the significance of this law and how crucial it is for kids. The speaker asked the official, "So, what exactly does this mean and what are your thoughts about how we accomplish this goal of leaving no child behind?" The official replied with some redundant rhetoric about the loftiness of the goal and how educators should take it very seriously and embrace it in order that all children reap the benefits. Two or three times the speaker asked the official for a precise explanation of the law and specific strategies for accomplishing its goals. After several minutes of bantering, hearing no definitive responses, the speaker concluded that few people, including many politicians, understand exactly what the law is asking for. Many have boarded the improvement bandwagon without knowing specifically what it looks like.

As honorable as it sounds, "Leave no child behind" is still an ambiguous proclamation. The bottom line is that educators are, and rightly should be, focused on helping every child learn. Appropriately using and understanding data can help in accomplishing that goal. We must decide what schools are about and what we expect them to accomplish. And we must be consistent in our use of data for helping every child learn.

In many states across the country, not only do targets change, but assessments change as well, providing little consistency in data that are usable from year to year. For example, since its inception the Indiana mandated assessment, the Indiana Statewide Testing for Educational Progress (ISTEP), has undergone a progression of changes. In 2002–2003, Indiana students were tested in grades 3, 6, 8, and 10. When the ISTEP was first introduced in 1988, it was administered to students in grades 1, 2, 3, 6, 8, 9, and 11 and used as a criteria for determining promotion and retention. By 1992, this practice had been discontinued when the testing of students in grades 2 and 11 was dropped. In the late 1990s the pass/fail criteria changed and an arbitrary scale score "cut" was established. There was little consistency in regard to where the cut score was set from one grade level to the next. This resulted in situations where students scoring above the established cut score as third graders could make what was believed to be adequate progress, then score below the cut score as a sixth grader. In an effort to establish greater consistency, the cut scores were readjusted in 2002. Furthermore, actual data used for reporting student performance changed from percentage correct to a performance index score. In some instances, the two contradicted one another in regard to the identification of strengths and weaknesses. Such inconsistencies are common throughout the country and only complicate the elusive criteria for determining "quality" schools.

This book is an attempt to help those who work with data share them and use them more effectively—or at least a bit more intelligently. It is intended to provide a means for creating stability in an ever changing field of targets.

1

CHOOSE TO DANCE, BUT . . .

Perhaps a key point to begin with is the premise that data don't lie, but they can be misunderstood and misinterpreted. When I began this dance with data several years ago, I knew that conventional standardized tests were being used to make high-stakes decisions. I was intrigued by the fact that data from these tests were being used to hold schools and teachers accountable. But I observed discrepancies between what educators were saying about students and what the tests were saying. What I heard from teachers was: "We're teaching it, but the tests seem to indicate they're not learning it."

I observed that many teachers paid little or no attention to data, partly because they didn't understand and partly because the data had neither meaning nor significance to them. I sometimes observed that secondary teachers viewed data from standardized tests as "the guidance counselor's responsibility." Once, as I was meeting with a committee of teachers working on curriculum issues, I asked how they used the standardized test data to determine strengths and weaknesses or to improve their instruction. A high school English teacher replied quite emphatically, "I don't have time to look at that data stuff. I have too much curriculum to cover!"

With the advent of a state-mandated graduation qualifying exam, however, I saw the tides turn. Middle and high school teachers started asking questions about the data. They began to recognize the significance of the data in reference to what they were teaching. More importantly, in light of the well-publicized data, some began to take a closer look at *how* they were teaching. The mantra of teachers and administrators became "The test's the thing!" (My apologies to Shakespeare and Hamlet.)

I decided to find out more about the topic of standardized testing. I chose to conduct a study that resulted in a doctoral dissertation focused on how data are used by teachers and administrators. My studies provided me with great insight into the evolution of the standardized test.

The issue of assessing student achievement is a complex one that has been studied from a variety of perspectives for a number of different reasons. The federal government seeks to find out if American schools are preparing students for global competition. Now they are insisting and have even legislated that "no child be left behind." At the state level, leaders compare achievement levels of their students with those of students across the country. The business community seeks answers as to why high school and college graduates are many times less than qualified to perform the jobs they have to offer. Parents want to know how effective their child's school is compared to the one across town. Teachers merely want to know what their students have learned.

Since its inception, formal assessment of students has undergone a number of changes throughout the United States. Not only have the underlying purposes of assessment changed but also the philosophy and methodology. These changes have been so drastic that the assessment of student achievement has become a subject from which much controversy has evolved.

The push for accountability has propelled this issue into a high-stakes game. Robert Marzano (Marzano, Pickering, & McTighe, 1994) suggests that the "back to basics" movement of the 1970s led to "an emphasis on low-level functional skills and the proliferation of minimum-competency tests." He identifies several factors that have contributed to the demands for assessment reform of the 1990s: (1) the changing nature of educational goals, (2) the relationship between assessment and teaching and learning, and (3) the limitations of current methods of recording performance and reporting credit.

While statewide testing began as far back as 1849 in Oregon, it did not become commonplace until 1929 when Iowa developed the Iowa

Every-Pupil Test. The Iowa test was initially used for a high school academic contest for the purpose of measuring educational achievement and stimulating interest in academics. By 1935, however, interest in the test had spread to other states across the country (Peterson, 1983).

Two notable events led to an increased interest in testing programs by a number of states. The launching of Russia's satellite *Sputnik* in 1957 led to significant changes in education across the country. The race was on—not only in regard to space travel but in the academically competitive world as well. According to M. W. Kirst (1979), "accountability statutes" were passed by 35 states between 1966 and 1976 and often included "new state tests and assessment devices that re-orient local curricula to the state tests" (p. 51). The most aggressive movement toward minimum competency testing took place between 1976 and 1978.

The second event was the 1983 publication of *A Nation at Risk* (1983), a 36-page open letter to the American people from the National Commission on Excellence in Education. Among other things, the report stated that test scores "indicated a persistent skills erosion in English, mathematics, and science among students including those in college" (dePaolo, 1993).

While the report served as a wake-up call for many aspects of public education, perhaps it provided a negative linkage of test scores to the measurement of school achievement. The practice of comparing test scores has become quite common as an apparent solution for identifying problems related to instruction and curriculum. In a 1994 report, Robert Glaser and Edward Silver point out that

> achievement measurement has become increasingly institutionalized and has been a focal point of attention on indicators of school effectiveness. However, much less attention has been paid to how assessments might be used to shape and improve learning and schooling . . . the integration of assessment and learning as an interacting system has been too little explored. (p. 14)

The National Research Council (NRC) (1989) reacted similarly regarding the area of mathematics: "As we need standards for curricula, so we need standards for assessment. We must ensure that tests measure what is of value, not just what is easy to test. If we want students to investigate, explore, and discover, assessment must not measure just mimicry mathematics" (p. 19).

According to studies conducted by the North Central Regional Educational Laboratory (NCREL), the primary purpose of assessment in public schools across the country is to improve instruction (Bond, 1997). Yet the same source suggests that most educators are not taught how to use the results of tests to improve instruction. Often, the receipt of test data in terms of scales scores, percentiles, and stanines is acknowledged, but no further analysis is attempted (Sanders & Horn, 1995).

In 1982 Eric Gardner cited five common misuses of standardized tests. While all five have validity, the fourth point, "lack of understanding of test score reporting" is significant to this book. Gardner states that there is substantial misunderstanding, not just among laymen but also among many educators, of the meaning of test scores. Most people believe that they understand the meaning of a raw score or of that particular raw score converted to a percentage of items answered correctly, as in the case of many criterion-referenced tests. However, even in this most elementary illustration, more is involved than a single number indicates. Gardner observes that the interpretation of a raw score converted to a percentile score causes even more problems, and the misinterpretation of grade equivalents is even more common. A grade equivalent is the score that was exceeded by 50 percent of the group at the specific time the test was given. It does not represent a standard to be attained. It does not represent the grade in which the pupil is functioning academically or should be placed, as is a common misunderstanding. Gardner advocates for increased efforts to train teachers on the principles of test construction and test interpretation.

The NCREL stresses the importance of reporting assessment results to interested individuals and groups so that their needs for information are met and they have a clear understanding of the assessment. They further point out that students, parents, and community members often misinterpret assessment data because they do not view the information in the proper context. The real goal of reporting assessment results to the students, parents, school, and the public is to help children learn. Yet this message is rarely reported or conveyed when schools release assessment results. The reason for this omission might be that some educators and policymakers are not fully aware of the different purposes for assessment. They may not know how to convey those purposes, as well as assessment results, to various audiences (Roeber, 1995).

Despite the current attention given to student assessment, relatively little has been written on the use and reporting of assessment results. Even less research exists on the effectiveness of alternative strategies for using and reporting student assessment results. Yet public reporting of large-scale assessment results generates some of the biggest complaints about student assessment (Roeber, 1995).

It is imperative that educators, legislators, and the public in general clearly understand the specific goals and purposes of assessment. They must know not only the purpose behind each type of assessment instrument but why various assessment instruments are being used. For example, the purposes of criterion-referenced tests are fundamentally and specifically different from the purposes of norm-referenced tests. Criterion-referenced tests measure achievement of specific criteria or skills, while norm-referenced tests indicate students' performance in relation to the performance of others. A basic understanding of the difference between the two is imperative if we expect educators to use test data appropriately and to effectively communicate test results to parents and community.

Pencils Down: A Guide for Using and Reporting Test Results is a pamphlet developed by the staff of the Michigan Educational Assessment Program in 1989 in connection with the Michigan Department of Education for the purpose of helping a school district and building staff use and report assessment results (Gucwa & Mastie, 1989). The development and use of the guide was based on several assumptions significant to the problem. Generally, educators have no formal training in testing. Those who have had courses on testing were taught more about test construction and reading test reports than about how to use the results to help plan for instruction. Without some in-service training, most educators find it difficult to use test results effectively and often become easily frustrated. Supplying teachers with practical ways for using test results for identifying needs for changes in curriculum and instruction provides meaning and validates the time they spend preparing for and administering tests.

It is evident that the stakes in regard to standardized test results are high. The general public, many parents, political leaders, and even some educators think that schools should be rated on the basis of their students' scores on standardized tests. An enormous problem has been created as teachers and administrators across the country work to improve scores by modifying curriculum and altering instructional practices. Glaser and Silver (1994) and others address the issue:

> Under current circumstances, assessment-driven instruction creates a dilemma for many good teachers for whom teaching within a narrowly circumscribed, assessment-defined space is not acceptable. Externally mandated assessments cannot be ignored, since the teachers, their students and their schools are likely to be judged on the basis of student achievement. Yet, teaching only the content of these assessments is also unacceptable. Several reports (e.g. Livingston, Castle, & Nations, 1989; McNeil, 1988) suggest that reform-minded teachers attempt to overcome the inadequacies of the system through a kind of "double-entry" curriculum and instruction in which they attempt to give sufficient attention to the narrow goals embodied in the external assessments without sacrificing instructional attention to deeper conceptual understandings or broader curricular goals. Although some teachers find ways to teach high-level content despite the pressures of external assessment, many do not. . . . Clearly, there is a need to address the current dysfunctionality by improving the interaction between assessment and instruction to ensure that these two facets of educational activity work in harmony rather than at cross purposes. (p. 17)

> The irony of the public demand for standardized test data is that it is based on blind faith in the accuracy of the data. Most teachers and parents do not understand how tests are designed, how scores are derived, or how data are to be interpreted. (Paris, 1991, p. 14)

With the advent of high stakes testing, *accountability* has become an increasingly significant word in the education arena these days. It has powerful and far-reaching effects on many people. With accountability comes enormous responsibility. It is important for lead educators to take responsibility for apprising and educating entire communities, both within and outside the school walls, about how decisions are made around the use of data. We need to become more proactive in regard to what others hear and read about what is happening (or not happening) in our schools. Furthermore, we need to take a proactive approach for educating the public and advocating for ourselves rather than reacting to accusations and criticism.

Educators are scrutinized by many. This game of accountability has many players. Parents look to identify the best schools and decide if their own local schools are good enough for their children. Legislators carry the sentiment of the public to assure their constituents that schools are improving and maintaining adequate degrees of quality. Local school boards follow the lead of state and national legislators to pledge to their communities that top-quality schools are maintained. The media bear the responsibility of reporting the truth to the public, a right built into our Constitution. As the key players, teachers are worried, stressed, concerned, and misunderstood. More often than not, they lack understanding of the rules. They are fearful that data will be used to judge them unfairly.

Accountability takes on different flavors and definitions depending upon the players. In this age of high-stakes testing, 49 of our 50 states prescribe a mandatory assessment. The collection and use of data by teachers and administrators has increased dramatically in recent years. Congruent to the use of data is the challenge and need for understanding the data.

Insufficient time and effort have been put forth to teach our educators to disaggregate, interpret, understand, and put these data to use in their daily classroom instruction. The use of data by teachers has not been a high expectation. As I travel to different cities throughout the country, helping teachers interpret and understand data, I often ask an assembled group, "If I needed it today, where could I find the results from your school's most recently administered standardized tests?" The answer I frequently encounter is, "Probably stuck in a closet or file drawer collecting dust." With this response, heads across the room nod in agreement. Then I ask, "When was the last time you looked at these reports?" Generally, the groups respond with chuckles, laughter, and an occasional look of guilt. The bottom line here is that such information is of no value unless we use it, and we don't use it unless we understand it.

Adequate time for professional development continues to be an issue with teachers and administrators. There is either too little time or too little emphasis necessary for making the time a priority. Teachers need to have time not only to learn but to reflect upon what they've learned. They must be provided opportunities for interacting with each other. Much too often a school's professional development plan, if one even exits, means sending a teacher to a one-day workshop once a year, and the teacher returns to the classroom with little or no expectation for putting into practice the information learned. Rarely does the plan call for follow-up or interacting with other teachers. Only by chance does any sharing take place.

One of my favorite quotes is, "If we always do what we always did, we'll always get what we always got." (The author of this adage is unknown to me.) We could modify this statement to address the issue of providing teachers with adequate opportunities for professional growth: if we allow teachers to attend only random acts of professional development, we'll get only random instances of professional growth.

We could learn a lot from a basketball coach. How does a coach use data? After all, the true coaches are teachers. They study the data of not only their own team but the opposing teams as well. And it's not a case of examining the data once a year and then putting the information on a shelf to collect dust. The data are of little value to the coach unless that information is current. Furthermore, coaches never limit their use of data to once every three or four years, or even annually. They tend to review the data after every game and often as frequently as after every practice. Their players are constantly changing; their skills improve through practice. A coach studies the data of each player, adjusts the instruction, lines out a plan for practice, and reevaluates at some point later to see if the instructional strategies have worked. Generally, coaches review the data with assistant coaches or managers. They study the information, reflect on it, then act according to what they learn. Shouldn't the classroom teacher be following similar rules when using data?

I challenge you to *choose to dance with data*. But keep in mind that when you do, you acquire an enormous responsibility. Choosing not to dance is irresponsible.

2

DON'T FOX TROT IN A DISCO: RECOGNIZE YOUR AUDIENCE

Several years ago, when I was first put in charge of curriculum and assessment for my school district, I had minimal experience explaining data to others. I had helped teachers understand standardized test data, but for the most part I knew very little about the topic. Basically, I knew little more than the difference between a "percentile" and "percentage." I learned from others and sought out my own resources.

The more I studied and learned, the more I recognized the necessity to tailor the information to different audiences. Each group has its own knowledge base. Each group has its own purposes for using the data. Each group therefore requires data presented in an appropriate genre. Here are some suggestions for tailoring explanations to meet the needs of various groups and individuals.

SCHOOL BOARDS

School boards can be key players in the use and understanding of data. They need basic knowledge of terms and a larger picture of what data mean relative to the school district. Getting them on board in understanding the data is essential. Teaching them appropriate use of those data is paramount. Often boards or individual board members understand the proverbial "just enough to make them dangerous." The nature of school boards provides them opportunities to use data to promote their political agendas and actions rather than to benefit kids. Providing them with basic knowledge and basic tools for understanding the data can help to ward off unjust and harmful misinterpretation.

Four simple rules can help convey the message effectively while keeping the messenger from getting shot: (1) make it clean, clear, and simple, (2) make it concise, (3) always present some good news, and (4) let them know what's being done about the bad news.

Make It Clean, Clear, and Simple

Unless they are very experienced or come from the world of educators, school board members may not understand the terminology and jargon that we consider commonplace. It is important that they have an opportunity to review the information prior to any presentation. No one likes to be embarrassed in public, be it the presenter or the audience, so they should have opportunities prior to a public meeting to ask questions and discuss issues related to the data. Providing them with data a few days ahead of the presentation allows them time to review, reflect, and prepare questions. It is a good idea to include a glossary with clearly defined terms and definitions as part of the presentation materials.

During the presentation, slides referencing key terms can serve to clarify and inform visually (see figures 2.1, 2.2, 2.3, and 2.4 on pages 11 and 12). The use of color coding and symbols can also help to discriminate among and clarify terms that may be confusing. For example, when referencing nationally normed data, show a symbolic U.S. map for examples (see figures 2.5 and 2.6 on page 13) and use a background color different from slides containing criterion-referenced data. If criteria data are based on state standards, use a state symbol or map. Use a white background for slides showing definitions. Slides explaining norm-referenced information should have the same background color as slides explaining criterion-referenced information. It is important to point out these features to the audience at the beginning of the presentation.

Compares the student's cognitive ability with that of students who are the same age.

CSI

Figure 2.1.   Cognitive Ability Index

Experience and common sense can help the presenter anticipate what questions might be asked or what issues might be important. However, if the presenter is unfamiliar with the group, doing some homework by talking and asking questions of the individual board members, building principals, or central office administrators will be preparation time well spent.

Adopted by the Indiana State Board of Education

Figure 2.2.   Academic Standards

Criterion-reference Information

State Standards

Student's scores relative to a *body of information* thought to be important to learn.

Figure 2.3.   Criterion-Reference Information

Criterion-reference

"Cut-off" standards are recommended to the State Board by state educators.

Figure 2.4.   Criterion-Reference

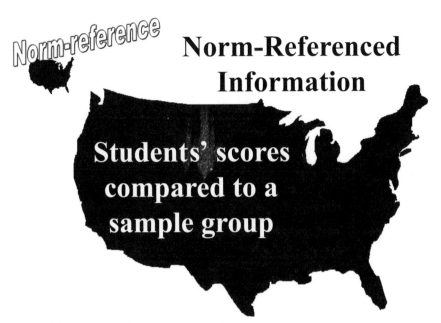

Norm-Referenced Information

Students' scores compared to a sample group

Figure 2.5.   Norm-Referenced Information

NCE & CSI Comparison 1995–1998

Grade 6 ISTEP ☐ Mean NCE				
	READ	LANG	MATH	BATT	CSI
CTBS/4 FCSC S 95	56.6	60.9	60.5	59.8	110.0
CTBS/4 FCSC S 96	57.8	62.8	60.9	61.1	111.0
CTBS/4 FCSC F 96	57.1	56.9	61.6	59.1	108.0
CTBS/5 FCSC F 97	59.3	59.7	54.5	57.9	107.0
CTBS/5 FCSC F 98	57.2	58.8	58.9	58.3	100.7

Grade 8 ISTEP ☐ Mean NCE				
	READ	LANG	MATH	BATT	CSI
CTBS/4 FCSC S 95	58.0	57.3	57.5	58.1	
CTBS/4 FCSC S 96	NT	NT	NT	NT	NT
CTBS/4 FCSC S 96	59.3	58.1	58.4	59.6	108
CTBS/5 FCSC S 97	60.6	56.6	57.9	58.4	108
CTBS/5 FCSC S 98	57.2	58.8	58.9	58.3	100.7

Figure 2.6.   NCE & CSI Comparison, 1995–1998

Here's one more little tip from someone who learned the hard way: don't forget to include page numbers for referencing during the presentation. It's a simple thing to do that will make the presentation easier on the audience as well as the presenter.

Make It Concise

The last thing board members need is to sit through a long, boring presentation of more information than they can really apply. Keep your presentation brief, and summarize as much of the information as possible. Use plenty of graphs and charts that are easy to understand, keeping the amount of information and data on each one to a minimum.

Graphs and charts need to be clear and well labeled as to:

- what is being represented
- what should be emphasized
- what is critical or exceptional

Here are more specific examples:

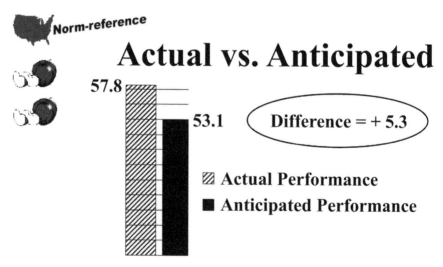

Figure 2.7. Actual vs. Anticipated Performance

Perhaps the most critical distinction when explaining data to any group, especially the school board, is to help them understand the differences between "apples and oranges" data. In this book I've included various examples and frequently provide pictures of apples and oranges on the document, chart, or visual to which I'm referring.

In these examples (figures 2.8 and 2.9), grade-level data are displayed. It is critical that the audience understands that different groups of students are being compared. Emphasize that scores from the sixth-grade class of 1996 represent a completely different group of students than the scores of the sixth-grade class of 1997. It appears simple, logical, and reasonable to those of us who work with and understand data, and we often assume that the audience understands the difference. Too often they do not, resulting in unfair comparisons and judgments.

Present the information in general terms as it relates to the district as a whole. Singling out weaknesses in specific buildings at public meetings can be potentially damaging and dangerous politically unless the data

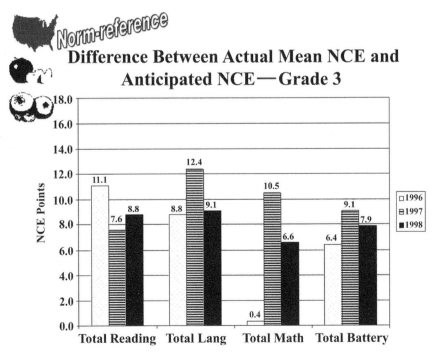

Figure 2.8.   Difference between Actual Mean NCE and Anticipated NCE—Grade 3

Criterion-reference

Percent of Students below State Cut-Off
1996–1998

| | Our School District | | | | | | | |
| | Grade 3 | | Grade 6 | | Grade 8 | | Grade 10 | |
	Lang. Arts	Math	Lang. Arts	Math	Lang. Arts	Math	Lang. Arts	Math
Sept 96	30%	36%	39%	41%	21%	40%	25%	36%
Sept 97	22%	19%	23%	35%	17%	22%	18%	39%
Sept 98	20%	29%	33%	41%	23%	34%	20%	37%
Difference	2%	-10%	-10%	-6%	-6%	-12%	-2%	2%

This chart compares three different groups of students.

Figure 2.9.   Percent of Students below State Cut Off, 1996–1998

are used to show how these entities have improved. Anticipate questions about specific buildings and groups and address them generally.

Always Present Some Good News

We're all human, so we all like to hear good news along with news about areas of concern. Be realistic, though, and be prepared to justify your findings—if not to inquisitive board members, then to probing newspaper reporters or parents who might be in the audience. Find ways to provide the board with optimism about progress, improvements, or comparisons. Sometimes this is difficult and requires some digging and analysis of different kinds of data, but it's rare that good news can't be found in any set of data.

Let Them Know What's Being Done about the Bad News

Bad news is inevitable, but necessary. It is unwise to paint a rosy picture about what is happening within the district when data that are less than flattering almost always exist. Board members want to be able to explain this information to their constituents easily and provide them with an explanation as to what is being done to correct problem areas. That way, when they're approached in the local grocery with negative comments or questions, they can share what is being done to address people's concerns. It will not only make the board member look informed, but it will add credibility to your work in preparing them.

PARENTS

While we sometimes believe that parents are not interested in learning about data, it is much more likely that they lack understanding of what the data mean. Parents want and deserve to understand data about their children. Parents need to be educated in regard to definitions, scores, and comparisons.

A survey was conducted to gauge parent perceptions about mandated state testing in 2000 by Harris Interactive in conjunction with Sylvan Learning Center and the Association for Supervision and Curriculum Development (Gleason, 2000). The survey findings among 600 Internet responses regarding parents' views include the following:

- Half are unsure of or do not know what the state standardized tests measure.
- Overall, parents do not feel informed about standardized assessment tests or equipped to help their children prepare for them.
- A majority does not believe mandated state testing is a true or valid measurement of what their children have learned.
- Nearly half find inconsistencies between their children's standardized test results and their report cards.

Data can be intimidating, and often parents don't know what they don't know, or they don't understand enough about the data to ask the right questions. If they do understand some of the data, our jargon and "alphabet soup" can be so confusing that they are too overwhelmed to ask questions. We have a responsibility to teach parents and to help them become comfortable with data. The better informed they are, the more likely they will be to take ownership as a solid partner in the education of their children.

A couple of years ago, a mother called to make an appointment to talk with me about the scores from her daughter's school. When she entered my office a couple of days later, she had in her hand a copy of the district's report card. This report card, required of each school district in the state, was a summary of state-mandated test scores, graduation and attendance rates, and other information. It was intended to be used as a means for parents and the general public to rate schools and judge their effectiveness.

I admired Ms. Smith for being concerned. I was pleased to see someone concerned enough about her child's school to take the time to not only question the data, but to seek the answers. I let her know that when she walked into my office.

She told me that she had read through the information in the report card carefully. While she was cordial, she was critical of the school system and troubled by the information. She began by saying, "We're getting worse! Look at these scores. I don't want my child going to a school that's losing ground. You're the director of curriculum. What are you doing about this problem?"

I asked her to provide me with specific questions about the data to which she was referring. She began, "Just look here." She pointed to the score indicating the percent of students who fell below the "passing" cut-off score on the state-mandated test for third-grade students. "Last year's score was six points higher than this year's. We're getting worse! What are you going to do to change that?"

DAILY LOCAL NEWS
Anywhere, USA

Local Third Graders Scores Drop

1999   23 percent of third graders fail state exam
2000   29 percent of third graders fail state exam

I explained to her that her example was an "apples to oranges" comparison. "They're not the same kids. You can't compare one class of students to another class." I had offered this explanation many times to a variety of different audiences, including parents. "You cannot compare one class of third-grade students to another. There are all kinds of variables that affect these scores. Different groups of students have differing abilities. Where one group of students may be strong in math computation skills, for example, the next group might not be. Students are at different places along the learning continuum and achieve at different rates." I assumed that I was getting through to her and that she was beginning to understand. I quickly discovered, however, that my assumptions were wrong.

"So why are our scores declining?" she asked. "What can be done to improve them? I don't want my kids to go to a school that is getting worse instead of better."

I continued to try to explain that it is very difficult—nearly impossible—to determine whether or not schools are improving based on these scores. "Scores from this test are not a good way to determine whether or not a group of students or a school is growing or improving," I said. "To determine that, there must be consistency in the measure, and testing must take place, using the same form of measurement, once or twice a year, and every year. This state-mandated test is only given to students at grades 3, 6, 8, and 10. You see, we won't see data like these for this group of third-grade students until they become sixth graders. We don't have the consistent data from this test to determine improvement." I continued to explain the "apples to oranges" issue. She continued to demand an answer as to why her child's school was getting worse instead of better.

For 45 minutes I worked at explaining that the scores of the third graders of 2000 should not be compared to the scores of the 1999 third-grade class. I wasn't getting through to her. She just didn't understand. Then I explained that last year's third-grade students are now fourth graders. I also reminded her of the school boundary realignment that had taken place the previous year. I explained that the make-up of the population in her child's school changed by 28 percent.

"Oh!" she exclaimed, "they're not the same kids! This report card is showing the scores of two different groups of students." Finally, she understood!

It had taken nearly an hour of one-on-one discussion to get this interested, intelligent, concerned mother to understand a simple concept. But this is an issue that we face constantly. We must be persistent in our efforts to help parents better understand what the data mean and continue to offer explanations that are on their own levels of comprehension. Had I merely shown her two photographs of two different groups of students, perhaps it would have made the concept clearer much sooner.

Over the years I've offered evening mini-workshop sessions for parents. The success of this was limited at best. I have found that parents are reluctant to give up even an hour in the evening to learn about test scores, unless they know that they will be able to obtain specific answers about how to help their own children improve their scores. There are ways, however, to get them on board.

My wife, Cheryl, is a third-grade teacher who makes a great effort to find ways to help parents better understand the test data. Of greater concern to her, however, is finding ways to help parents understand and buy into the standards and skills over which her students are tested. Recently she enlisted the help of the other teachers and paraprofessionals in her school and came up with an idea for helping parents to understand the data and standards and to involve them in the learning process with their children.

Teachers, paraprofessionals, and the principal in her building look at a variety of data as they prepare their students for the state-mandated achievement test that is given to students in the fall of their third-grade year. Since state testing is given at the beginning of the school year, second-grade teachers are especially intentional about the use of data for improving their students' skills. They rely heavily on the RIT (Rasch Unit) scores from the Northwest Evaluation Association (NWEA) Measures of Academic Progress (MAP).

The NWEA RIT scale is an equal-interval scale that serves as a measure for academic growth. It provides a snapshot of the student's performance. Typically the assessment is administered to students in the fall and again in the spring. This results in "growth" data for each student. Because MAP is a computer-adaptive test, it designs a test unique for each student based on the student's ability to answer the questions.

Since the state-mandated tests are given at the beginning of grade three, the second-grade teachers look at the test data to help prepare their students. They use a variety of data, but specifically NWEA RIT scores. These scores are used as a predictor of sorts to determine which students may be less likely to pass the state exam. These data are used alongside other indicators such as scores from their reading and math programs, as well as the data-driven Accelerated Reader (AR®) program and teacher-made assessments. Based on this information, students are grouped into three categories. In the spring, the principal sends letters to the parents accordingly.

Students are grouped using the following criteria:

Students scoring in a medium to higher range—the school suggests that if the students read regularly and review math skills including math facts over summer, they should do well on the fall exam.

Students scoring in the low to average ranges—these students are urged to do extra work on reading and math skills over the summer in order for them to maintain the skills they have.

Students targeted as unlikely to pass—these students are provided with prescriptive plans for improvement, which may include tutoring, summer school, and other research-based remedial strategies. The schools follow up with these strategies throughout the fall.

Included in each letter is an invitation strongly urging parents to attend a meeting in May. Child care is provided. At this meeting teachers spend about 45 minutes revisiting the standards booklet sent home earlier in the school year. They reference the book by pointing out a few of the specific standards to refresh parents' memories. They also provide parents with a packet of summer math, reading, and language activities directly correlated to the standards. Included in the packet are refrigerator magnet "pockets" which hold strips each containing simple activities, such as "Measure your shoe and another shoe in your house, in inches and centimeters, then compare them." Another part of the packet is a test-preparation booklet with activities correlated with the school's reading program. It includes stories, comprehension questions, and test tips written on the students' reading level so that a child could do it alone or with parents' help. Either way, even if they "played school," they could benefit.

Records are kept of the parents who attend the meeting. Those who do not are given a second opportunity, this time only with the principal, who explains the procedure. Parents still not attending receive a phone call from the principal.

In addition, during the month of May teachers persistently urge their students to plan for summer reading and join summer library programs. They are encouraged to read AR-leveled books so that they can use the data to monitor their progress. Even though no AR tests are given to students during the summer, twice during the summer parents are provided with check-in times when they can meet with a teacher who can answer their questions and make additional recommendations.

When students return to school in the fall, teachers hold celebrations for those who have completed their packets. Within the first week, the school hosts a chili supper get-together—"Stepping into Standards"—for third-grade students and their parents. The parents are provided with a list of their child's grade-level standards. Teachers lead parents to activity centers where they have an opportunity to work through packets with activities centered on standards. If their child is having trouble with a standard, they highlight it on the list. Stations are divided into language arts and math groups. Sample pre-tests are available. At the language arts station, kids actually take a written test similar to what is found on the state test. Parents are encouraged to observe rather than assist their child.

During the same week, students write stories in class similar to what is expected on the state test. Sample anchor papers with rubrics are available for parents to review to help them understand how they are scored and the data are obtained.

They then move to a computer lab where the students demonstrate to their parents how they worked through an AR test they had taken on a story they read earlier that day. Students explain the program using two different sets of data—one in relation to their own reading level and one relative to the third-grade reading level. This activity provides data that parents as well as the students can understand and gives parents a better understanding of where their child is performing relative to other third-grade kids.

Checksheets listing the activities are color coded for easy sorting. Each activity is clearly marked in regard to standards, using the same wording as in the state standards documents, to help parents better understand and to develop a common language as a way to connect standards to activities.

This process provides a safe, nonthreatening way to help parents see the importance of data, and it gives them a clearer picture of what the data mean. It's a definite way to say to parents, "Here is what your kids are doing, here is what they need to know, here is what we're helping them with, and here are some ways you can help."

Whenever possible, parents need to be provided with a glossary of terms that are easy to understand. We must never assume that parents understand, or that they do not have the capacity to learn. In order to cultivate a true partnership between home and school, we should make every effort to help parents learn to speak the same language relative to data.

STUDENTS

Can we expect students to understand their test data? Absolutely! If we are to expect students to become responsible for their own learning, we must assume the responsibility of helping them understand data and develop their own learning goals based on data. While we are hearing more these days about data-driven decision making, I am often disappointed to learn that we're failing to involve students in the process. Sometimes we fail to give students enough credit in regard to their achievement data. If we don't expect them to understand, they won't.

A few years back I surveyed the teachers in my district to see how well they understood and used Achievement Level Test data in their classrooms. Two of the items on the survey were (1) "I discuss my students' ALT (NWEA) data with them," and (2) "My students understand ALT data." While I shouldn't have been surprised, I found that only 13 percent of the teachers believed that their students understood the data. Furthermore, only 37 percent of the teachers spent time discussing the data with their students. The results are shown in figures 2.10 and 2.11. Response choices were: SD = Strongly Disagree, D = Disagree, N = Neutral, A = Agree, and SA = Strongly Agree.

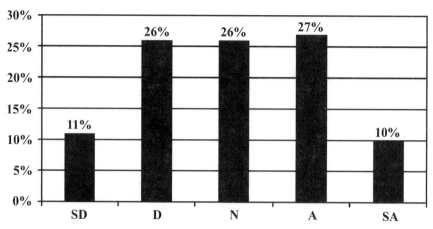

Figure 2.10.   I Discuss My Students' ALT Data with Them

I was amused and pleased with one of the written responses to the item about discussing students' data with them when a teacher replied, "No, but I will now!" Obviously, until the expectation was identified to her, she had not considered how she might empower her students by spending a few minutes explaining what the data mean.

Students of all ages possess the ability to learn about their own academic achievement and can set and achieve their own learning goals. I've observed in many kindergarten and first-grade classrooms teachers teaching their students how to graph. A common example is graphing

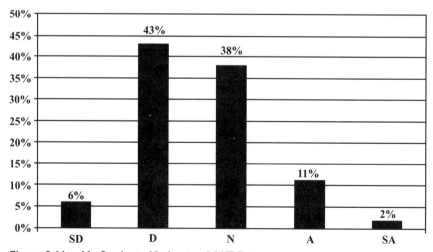

Figure 2.11.   My Students Understand ALT Data

Data Check Name _____ Date _____

Data Check Dates			
Grade Level			
AR Level			
Number of Books I Read Since Last Check			
NWEA RIT Scores			
Math			
Reading			
Language			
State Standardized Test Scale Scores			
Math			
Reading			
Writing			
Language			
Comments			

Figure 2.12.   Data Check

the number of red, yellow, brown, blue, and green M&Ms. We teach them about data early, so shouldn't we also be teaching them to apply these skills to track their academic progress?

As I work with teachers around the country, I hear numerous stories about how eager their students are to learn how much progress they have made from one testing season to another. This only happens, however, when they understand the numbers. When they are directly involved in setting their own target scores, they become even more engaged.

Simple forms can be developed by teachers for students to use to help track their own grades, test scores, and academic growth. An example is shown in figure 2.12.

ADMINISTRATORS

Never assume that administrators know and understand. An administrative license doesn't make a person an expert in statistics or interpreting test data. Much has changed since they took that one required graduate-level class years earlier (and probably much more has been forgotten than remembered).

Administrators need:

- help understanding what data mean
- time to interpret, assimilate, and discuss data
- simple explanations, charts, and graphs
- assistance in explaining information to teachers and developing plans to address concerns

Understanding What Data Mean

Merely sending an e-mail or memo is no assurance that the material will be read. Follow-up is critical, as are clear explanations about what is expected. Easy-to-understand examples and definitions are necessary. Earlier in this chapter I shared examples of ways for explaining terms and data to school boards. These work equally well with administrators.

Furthermore, *expecting* administrators to do something with their data is paramount—the more specific the better. When giving them the data, ask them to examine and analyze the information. Provide them with a task to complete that is relevant and meaningful—and provide them with an expected timeline. If a due date isn't included with the task, it is much less likely that anything will happen. And the task should not be busy work! Rather, it should be an activity that will provide them with a meaningful result that is relevant to a need, or to a building or district goal.

For example, ask them to compile a list of students who missed 15 or more days of school last year and compare the achievement growth of these students to the students who missed fewer than three days. In order to pique their interest in learning more, make it simple enough so that it doesn't take a large amount of time. The intent is for them to want to dig deeper and look at other factors.

Time to Interpret, Assimilate, and Discuss Data

Too often we use the excuse "I just haven't had the time to look at these data." I suggest that we rephrase that statement to "I just haven't *taken* the time to look at these data." We all have the same number of hours in every day. No one has given us an extra hour to look at data. Even if we did have that luxury, we might find something else to do during that hour unless we had established this activity as a priority. Administrators need help understanding the relevance in order for it to be on their high-priority list.

Establish regular meeting times to review and discuss their observations. Provide clarification for unfamiliar or confusing concepts or vocabulary. Be intentional and clear about expectations in order for the meetings to be productive.

Simple Explanations, Charts, and Graphs

Many administrators do not have the expertise or the inclination to develop elaborate charts and graphs. Encourage them to elicit the help of a teacher or assistant they probably know who may enjoy this kind of activity.

There is value to assisting them in creating their own charts and graphs. However, when feasible and realistic, provide them with simple charts and graphs already developed with their own data. The more time required the less apt they are to prepare their own, especially if they are uncomfortable or unskilled in doing so. In contrast, if you take every opportunity you have to teach and coach them in the skills and processes, the more likely they are to take the time to begin developing their own visuals.

Explaining Information to Teachers and Developing Plans to Address Concerns

Perhaps one of the best ways to help administrators "make it happen" is to provide them with a simple graphic organizer, such as the example I've included in figure 2.13. It is critical that administrators take the time to develop a diagram for using their data—something that's simple and concrete.

The "Taking Action" document provides them with a means to identify *what* needs to happen; *who* is to be involved either in presenting, studying, collecting, analyzing, teaching, printing, or receiving the data; and *when* each step is to happen. The "when" is an essential component in order for the plan to move to realization.

Taking Action

Action plan for _____ *Date* _____

Step	**What?** What needs to happen?	**Who?** Who is responsible for making it happen?	Who is to be involved?	**When?** When is this step to be completed	**Stepping Stones** What are potential roadblocks with strategies for preventing/overcoming?	**Resources** What resources are needed (materials &/or people)?	**Success!** How will we know when we are successful?
1							
2							
3							
4							
5							

Figure 2.13.   Taking Action Graphic Organizer

Perhaps the most important element of the plan, however, is the anticipation of and preparation for overcoming *roadblocks*. One roadblock common to everyone is that of time. Certainly strategies for developing realistic timelines are crucial, as are provisions for teachers and staff to have adequate time to study data and implement strategies for using them.

It is a good idea to identify *resources*, those needed as well as the ones readily available, as a part of the plan. Resources might be tangible, such as documents and reference material, or human resources needed to assist in teaching the staff how to use data effectively.

Finally, it is important to identify and establish measures for determining success. Such measures will help to provide results and avoid the discouragement of "going through the motions" with nothing to show for all of the effort.

TEACHERS

We are in an era where data are abundant. Furthermore, data are being used profusely for a variety of purposes by our public—parents as well as politicians. Some of the data are less than appropriate or unfair conclusions. Teachers are a direct link to the public and are needed to help the public understand the meaning of the data. Misinformation often spawns misinformation. Likewise, when teachers have good information, have knowledge, and are confident, the potential for impacting the public is immense in helping overcome misuse and misinformation around data.

As with administrators, never assume that teachers know and understand. In 1998 I conducted a study of 500 Indiana teachers and principals to determine:

- how effectively standardized test data are used by teachers and principals
- what kinds of decisions are made using these data
- teachers' and principals' knowledge in regard to these data

The study determined that teachers and administrators lack basic understanding of standardized test data. Given a seven-item test of terms and basic knowledge about standardized test data, 63 percent of the overall group failed.

As an example, participants were asked to respond to the statement, "Norm-referenced data (data relative to a sample group of students) are more useful information in regard to what I teach than criterion-referenced data (data relative to a body of information thought to be important to learn)." At the time, state standards and essential skills were heavily emphasized as the basis for the major portion of the state test, ISTEP+, yet only a small majority (52.8 percent) of all of the respondents said that they believed that criterion-referenced data were more useful to them in regard to what they taught than norm-referenced data.

To state that teachers are extremely busy people is a gross understatement. They reign as the sovereign multitaskers who continually strive to find better and more efficient ways of accomplishing their multitude of tasks and responsibilities. It is paramount that teachers are supported in their efforts to use data to improve the instruction in their classrooms. It must become a priority. Teachers, as do administrators, lament about not having the time to study and use data. But finding and making time is imperative. Teachers have a responsibility and obligation to understand and use data in order to improve learning for their students.

Perhaps one of the most effective ways to instill the importance of using data is to model using the information and embed its use into the culture of the school. Lip service alone by well-intentioned administrators won't cut it. Administrators and teacher leaders must embrace data and expect them to be used. Teachers must see the relevance. Furthermore, they must observe the use of data being modeled and expected.

Teachers also need a vehicle for sharing and learning from each other. No longer can we allow them to shut their doors and ignore what others are doing. Data provide a common language and an opportunity to share in the ownership for learning. Data from a grade level, building, or district can lead to collaborative activities. The concept of groups of teachers observing, learning, discussing, and critically analyzing data is powerful. Such activities lend themselves to building strategies for improving learning for kids.

NEWS MEDIA

As a district testing coordinator, I was responsible for administering the state-mandated standardized achievement test. One of my responsibilities was to answer questions from reporters and interpret the results of our district's tests. During my early years in this position, we would receive scores for our district at the same time they were being released to the media, leaving no time to digest the data before we were inundated with questions from the local reporters. Needless to say, this resulted in some stuttering and stammering as we tried to interpret the data while simultaneously answering such questions as "Why are your sixth-grade scores so low?" In more recent years, state departments of education have withheld the release of such data to the media until local districts have had at least a few days to digest them. This gives us a few days to try to anticipate some of their questions and to come up with intelligent answers.

Over the years, I became more cognizant of the intent behind the news media's inquiries and more confident in my responses. I became so bold that I began to respond to their questions with questions. One conversation with a local reporter went something like this:

"Hi, Dave. It's Mary, the education reporter from the local newspaper. I understand the state test results were released this week. How did your district do?"

"In regard to what specifically, Mary?"

"In regard to your test scores?"

"Specifically, which scores are you referring to, Mary? Are you wanting information about just certain subject areas?"

"Just mainly your district's scores."

"But which scores are you wanting information about? The norm reference scores or the criterion reference scores?

"Oh, er . . . well I guess the norm reference scores."

"Do you want to discuss the actual scores, anticipated scores, NCEs, or percentiles?"

"Um, well . . . I just want to know how your schools' scores look this year."

"Which grades do you want to discuss, Mary? Grade 3, 6, 8, or 10? In regard to how last year's classes performed, in regard to how this year's sixth-grade students performed compared to their scores as third graders?"

"Well, uh . . . Dave . . . I'm not sure. Let me talk to my editor and I'll get back with you."

"No problem, Mary. I look forward to talking to you soon."

This was not a case of my trying to get smart with the reporter (well, maybe I was just a little). She was one whom I respected and talked to often. But I wanted to make the point with her that these data cannot be generalized. Furthermore, rarely can they be used to compare one class to the next in a shallow manner. Too often the news media choose to rank schools based on scores they know little or nothing about. They rank one school against another with little or no regard to the differences among the students from one school to the next. (In chapter 3, I will describe ways to look at and explain comparative data.)

It was not long after my discussion with Mary that I contacted the other test coordinators in our area and asked them if they would be willing to meet with the local reporters as a group, but not just to report the scores. I suggested presenting a workshop about how to interpret the scores and explain exactly what they mean. Shown in figures 2.14, 2.15, and 2.16 are examples of some of the information we shared.

We provided them with definitions and explanations of our scores. During one of the first meetings we talked about the fact that it is unfair to compare one school to another, to compare this year's sixth-grade class to last year's—that they are two completely different groups of students. During the session I asked the reporters *not* to rank schools in regard to their scores. "It's an unfair comparison," I pointed out.

"Oh, we have to publish those lists," they replied. "The public expects it! It's the only way they can understand how one school differs from another."

Although the public may expect it, they have no idea what it really means. It's an "apples and oranges" comparison. It was then I realized that we, as educators, had to take the responsibility to educate the reporters.

I challenged one reporter to use "apples and oranges comparison" in the story's headline. I knew that while he was responsible for writing the story, his editors were likely responsible for the headlines, so I was not really expecting my challenge to come to fruition. However, I was pleasantly surprised the next day when the headline read: "Educators say comparing schools can be misleading. Process amounts to 'apples and oranges' because varying factors exist, official stresses" (McCleery, 2001). I was delighted and made sure to praise the reporter on his accomplishment. It was a small but important step toward helping them understand.

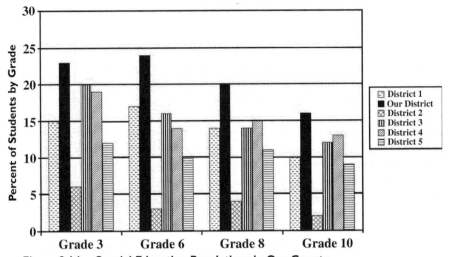

Figure 2.14. Special Education Populations in Our County

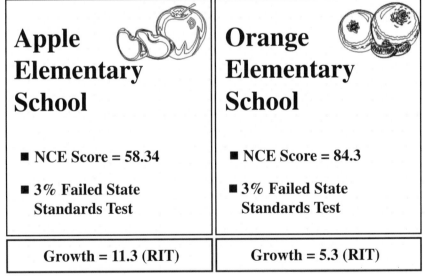

Figure 2.15. Apple Elementary School vs. Orange Elementary School

Indiana Academic Standard Summary

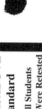

Corporation	Grade	Percent BELOW CUT-OFF Lang. Arts	Math	Percent ABOVE Standard GQE	All Students Who Were Retested Lang. Arts	Math
District 1	3	19%	15%			
	6	29%	23%			
	8	18%	22%			
	10	13%	14%	Retest	35%	58%
District 2	3	31%	27%			
	6	40%	27%			
	8	26%	38%			
	10	26%	29%	Retest	43%	56%
District 3	3	36%	33%			
	6	49%	35%			
	8	30%	25%			
	10	45%	38%	Retest	41%	66%
OUR DISTRICT	3	35%	28%			
	6	47%	36%			
	8	28%	34%			
	10	29%	29%	Retest	48%	45%
District 4	3	28%	19%			
	6	41%	23%			
	8	19%	27%			
	10	26%	22%	Retest	51%	66%
District 5	3	21%	22%			
	6	38%	29%			
	8	22%	29%			

Median NCE

School	Grade	Total Reading	Total Language	Total Math	Total Battery
District 1	3	65.0	67.3	74.6	70.6
	6	64.7	64.2	63.6	64.7
	8	62.5	61.8	65.2	63.2
	10	Did not administer			
District 2	3	57.1	60.4	64.1	60.3
	6	60.0	62.2	67.1	63.2
	8	58.0	56.7	56.9	55.9
	10	58.3	57.4	61.9	58.6
District 3	3	57.9	62.3	58.9	61.4
	6	56.5	54.1	58.3	55.6
	8	57.8	61.0	66.0	62.0
	10	48.7	52.7	55.5	53.5
OUR DISTRICT	3	59.4	62.7	63.3	62.0
	6	55.9	56.0	61.0	57.8
	8	59.4	56.1	56.5	57.3
	10	Did not administer			
District 4	3	60.4	63.8	76.7	66.3
	6	60.0	59.3	67.1	61.9
	8	61.7	64.8	62.1	63.8
	10	Did not administer			
District 5	3	60.9	62.6	57.4	61.6
	6	60.8	57.3	69.5	62.4
	8	58.0	53.8	62.0	56.7

Figure 2.16. Our County Indiana Fall 2000 ISTEP+

DON'T TRIP OVER YOUR OWN FEET: NEVER ASSUME THEY KNOW

"**N**ever assume anything" and "Base your decisions on facts" are two pieces of very sound advice. Never assume that people understand what you've told them, what you've tried teaching them, or what you believe they should have learned somewhere along the way. People often are afraid to ask questions for fear of coming across as ignorant or foolish.

When presenting data to groups or individuals, I have found it helpful to provide a glossary with frequently used terms or terms that are often confusing to people. I have found an excellent glossary of terms at the website of the Association for Supervision and Curriculum Development, www.ascd.org/cms/objectlib/ascdframeset/index.cfm?publication= http://ascd.org/publications/books/1996hibbard/glossary.html.

I have observed that the terms *norm reference* and *criterion reference* can be confusing, and I am often asked to explain the difference "just one more time." I clarify the difference by using a map of the United States and suggesting that the word *norm* be associated with *national*, as norming studies used for these data typically are derived from nationwide norm groups. An effective practice to help people remember *criterion*, on the other hand, is to use a graphic representative of the criteria against which pieces of data are being judged.

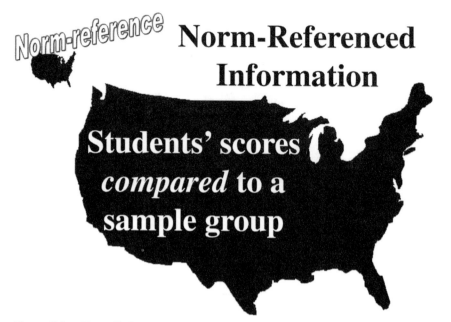

Norm-Referenced Information

Figure 3.1. Norm-Referenced Information

In my 1998 study of teachers' and administrators' knowledge of test interpretation terms, one of most common concerns I determined was that nearly half of the educators surveyed were using norm-referenced data as the basis for their instructional decisions, rather than criterion-referenced data based on the state standards.

APPLES AND ORANGES ARE DIFFERENT FRUITS

In chapter 2, I referenced the proverbial apples to oranges comparison. I refer to these pictures often in presentations. It is a simple, familiar way to help others see how and how not to compare points of data.

Perhaps one of the most abused comparisons that I have observed is when grade-level data are compared from one year to another. For example, one might try to gauge improvement by comparing the scores of fourth-grade students from the spring of 2000 to the scores of fourth-grade students in the spring of 2001. This is a prime example of an apples to oranges comparison. Obviously, the fourth-grade class of 2000 is a completely different group of students than the fourth-grade class of 2001.

A more accurate and fair way, if we choose to compare scores from one year to the next, is to use *cohort* information. Cohort data are consistent data gathered from the same students year after year. Too often, consistency of data is ignored. It is extremely difficult to compare year-to-year growth unless factors that influence the data are consistent from year to year. Such factors as mobility, types of data, and differences in criteria can make significant differences. Take, for example, two groups of students—the Green Group and the Red Group.

The Green Group of 83 fourth-grade students were tested using a criterion-referenced standardized achievement test in the spring of 2000. Based on scale scores, 79 percent of the Green Group students scored above the state-established cut score. The next spring, when the students were fifth graders, 86 percent scored above the cut score (see figure 3.1).

If we look only at the percentage passing, we would be led to believe that these students improved by 7 percent. However, if we look at the consistency factors, we find two significant differences:

1. In 2000 there were 83 students in the Green Group; in 2001 there were only 71 students in the Green Group. Of the 71 students, four students had moved into the district since the previous spring. Therefore, only 67 students were common to both years.
2. The cut score for fourth-grade students was set at a different level from the cut score for fifth-grade students. Specifically, students performing at the fourth-grade cut-score level performed near the 45th percentile when compared to peers in the nationally normed group; students performing at the fifth-grade cut-score level were near the 56th percentile. There was obvious inconsistency in determining cut scores from grade level to grade level.

We might say this comparison is like comparing Red Delicious to Granny Smith apples. In order to reasonably compare the year-to-year data to detemine improvement, we would need to compare like or

Table 3.1.   Green Group Testing

Green Group Season	Number of Students	Grade Level	Percentage Passing
Spring 2000	83	4	79 percent
Spring 2001	71	5	86 percent

matched students—those who took the test in 2000 who also took the test in 2001. Furthermore, we would need to establish cut scores that provide consistency from year to year.

Now, let's consider the Red Group: 83 fourth-grade students who were tested using an adaptive test designed to meet established criteria in the spring of 2000. As determined from a nationwide norm group, 79 percent of the Red Group students scored at a level typical of fourth-grade students. The next spring, when the students were fifth graders, 86 percent scored at a level typical of fifth-grade students, as determined from the same nationwide norm sample. Furthermore, only the data from like (matched) students were used. While other factors may have influenced these scores, the comparative data are based on much more stable conditions than with the Green Group.

Figure 3.2 is an example of how data from a cohort group can be used to compare student performance in mathematics determined by a subtest in the area of geometry. The example shows data from the same group of students from six testing cycles over three grade-level years:

- Grade 3, fall 1998 to spring 1999
- Grade 4, fall 1999 to spring 2000
- Grade 5, fall 2000 to spring 2001

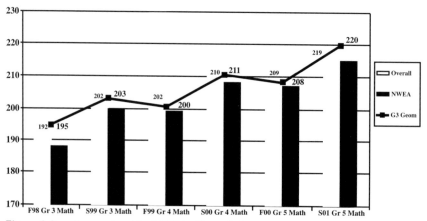

Figure 3.2. Comparing Goal RIT to Overall Average Math RIT—Goal 3—Geometry

For each testing season, the graph illustrates three points of data based on like students:

1. The overall math score for the group (dark bar)
2. The norm or typical group average (light bar)
3. The score of the group on the geometry subtest (line)

When presenting data to various groups of people, as outlined in chapter 2, simple examples help to more effectively paint a picture. Each time we share information provides a "teachable moment," an opportunity to educate the public about data.

ALWAYS ASK

Whenever in doubt—ask! Some years ago I read a book that focused on asking the right questions at the appropriate times. It taught me that sometimes even the obvious questions need to be asked. My father was a great teacher who used a quote in his classroom that I often use when making presentations: "He who asks is a fool for a minute; he who never asks is a fool forever." I presume that the quote is a modification of Abraham Lincoln's famous quote, "'Tis better to be silent and be thought a fool, than to speak and remove all doubt." Likewise, author

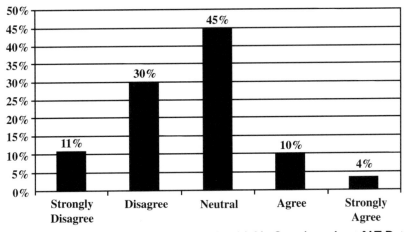

Figure 3.3. My Principal Has Provided Help with My Questions about ALT Data

Stephen Covey teaches us: "Seek first to understand, then to be understood."

No better advice can be found when helping people understand the principles of assessment data. Simple surveys can be valuable tools for determining needs and checking for understanding. In chapter 2 I referenced a survey given to teachers to determine how they were using Achievement Level Test data. Shown in figure 3.3 is a graph from the survey to determine how well they understood and used their test data.

The results of this question are obvious—the principals in the district were not viewed as helpful in answering their teachers' questions about test data. More frustrating to me, however, was realizing that I had spent many hours with principals, teaching them about data and how to work with their teachers. It was obvious that this model was not producing the results we wanted. Had we not asked, we would have continued to assume that the information was filtering down through them as designed.

Simple surveys (see figure 3.4) can provide quick, pertinent data for administrators. The key is to keep them *short* and *simple*. Long, detailed surveys—several pages long—only frustrate teachers and often are tossed before they're completed. If done right, one-page surveys are simple to complete, simple to compile, and can provide excellent feedback. In *The School Portfolio Tool Kit: A Planning, Implementation, and Evaluation Guide for Continuous School Improvement*, author Victoria Bernhardt provides some excellent guidelines for developing and conducting effective surveys.

I have included a sample of the survey mentioned above. Note that teachers were given three options for completing the survey, which was sent via e-mail. They could:

1. print it out and fill it out by hand.
2. fill in the appropriate boxes and return it via e-mail as an attachment.
3. pick up a hard copy of the survey from the school office.

You may (1) print this survey and fill it out by hand, (2) fill in the appropriate boxes and return it via e-mail as an attachment, or (3) pick up a printed survey from your school office.
PLEASE RETURN TO _____ **BY** _____. Thank you for your input!

Grade Level: ☐   Subjects Taught: ☐   Building: ☐

I have been teaching (✔) 1–3 years ☐   4–10 years ☐   11–15 years ☐   16+ years ☐

		Strongly Agree	Agree	Neutral	Disagree	Strongly Disagree
1.	I use the data from Achievement Level Tests (ALT).					
2.	Information from ALT is useful information.					
3.	Achievement Level Testing is worthwhile.					
4.	Analyzing ALT data has caused me to think about changing the way I teach.					
5.	How the data can be used has been adequately explained to me.					
6.	I would like to learn more about using ALT data.					
7.	Teachers in my building need more information about using ALT data.					
8.	FCSC Achievement Level Tests are aligned to my curriculum.					
9.	After studying the ALT data I have changed the way I teach.					
10.	After studying the ALT data I have changed what I teach.					
11.	My students understand ALT data.					
12.	ALT data provide an accurate picture of what my students can do.					
13.	My principal has provided help with my questions about ALT data.					
14.	I discuss my students' ALT data with them.					
15.	In my building teachers on my grade level/team find this data useful.					
16.	Use of ALT data has caused increased learning in my classroom.					
17.	Parents understand this data.					
18.	ALT data have been helpful in developing my annual instructional goals.					
19.	I am interested in learning more about how using ALT data might help change my classroom instructional strategies.					

Comments: (use other side, if needed)

Figure 3.4 Sample Survey

4

DON'T STOP WHEN YOU'RE TIRED—JUST CHANGE YOUR ROUTINE: USE IT OR LOSE IT, AND MAKE SURE YOUR PARTNERS DO, TOO

Professional development for teachers is an honorable-sounding buzz phrase these days, and there are many effective professional development plans in place. Allowing teachers to pursue the proverbial concept of life-long learning is a cause few people can fault. Professional development is strongly encouraged by professional organizations, administrators, and politicians, and it is even supported by legislation and funding in some states. Yet "typical" professional development is relatively ineffective. It goes something like this:

- Teacher sees eye-catching workshop flier in workroom.
- Teacher fills out proper paperwork and submits it to principal.
- Principal approves the workshop and hires substitute teacher.
- Teacher spends hours preparing for substitute.
- Teacher attends one-day workshop.
- Teacher returns to classroom next day eager to try new, exciting, innovative, and creative ideas and techniques.
- Teacher implements one or two of the ideas.
- Teacher shares an idea with a couple of colleagues at lunch.
- Within a week or two, teacher has forgotten most of what was presented in the workshop.

- If we're lucky, teacher continues to use one or two of the concepts learned through the remainder of the school year.

The investment of time, money, and human resources was significant for this one-day, in-service opportunity. Yet comparatively, the results and impact on change was negligible at best. While the teacher may have learned some valuable ideas and may even have shared a couple of them with other teachers, it is unlikely that there was much of a lasting effect on many students.

DEVELOP A PLAN—THEN FOLLOW UP

Little change takes place as a result of the content of a workshop, no matter how good it is. Change and improvement result only when a well-developed, well-articulated plan is executed before, during, and most importantly *after* the professional development "events." If expectations are clearly developed and articulated before professional development events and a plan is in place for adequate follow-up, the likelihood of successful change and improvement increases significantly.

In planning for effective professional development and follow-up, we must ask ourselves several pertinent questions:

1. What are the anticipated outcomes?
2. What are the expectations of the teacher prior to attending?
3. How is this aligned with goals—personal/professional, building, or district?
4. What follow-up is expected?
5. Are teachers expected to report findings to anyone?
6. Are teachers expected to share the information at a faculty meeting; team, department, or grade-level meeting; or during an in-service day?
7. What long-range expectations are in place for follow-up, review of the information, and further training?

A clearly developed and well-articulated plan is necessary in order for change and improvement to happen. Expectations and follow-up are essential. When teachers are provided with professional opportunities, we need to ask such questions as:

1. What did they learn?
2. What opportunities are available for sharing their new learnings with others?
3. How are they being held accountable for what they learned?

Shown in figure 4.1 is an example of a planner for making professional development activities more effective.

One scenario for effectively using this planning sheet might look something like this:

- Principal and other teachers on the team establish goals based on data.
- Team, based on data, decides needed training for the team and establishes goal for becoming trained.
- Team designates a lead teacher who will attend training and, in turn, train the team.
- Team researches professional development opportunities.
- Team plans implementation for short-range (three months) and long-range (three years).
- Lead teacher attends training.
- Lead teacher returns, debriefs with team, and establishes dates for sharing, reflection, discussion, and implementation.
- Team implements plan and plans for future professional development.

In chapter 2, I introduced the *Taking Action* planning sheet, which can be used for "big picture" planning or for team planning. This sheet includes key questions that should address whatever planning is to take place.

In his article "Six Ways to Immediately Improve Professional Development," Dennis Sparks (2000) suggests that

the long-term goal must be a redesigned teacher workday which enables genuine team work and the informal learning that occurs when teachers spend time each day helping one another plan lessons, critique student work, and solve the common problems of teaching. Every school in the nation can begin this school year by planning worthwhile professional development experiences.

Date:

Team:		
1. Based on data, what are the professional development needs?		
2. What are the anticipated outcomes—short range (3 months) & long range (3 years)?		
3. What established building goal(s) does this address?		
	Date Notes	
Training(s) Identified		
Lead Teacher Identified		
Training	Outline of Key Points:	
Team Debrief Meeting		
Team Implementation Expectations 1. 2. 3. 4.	Date due	
Follow-up Needed 1. 2. 3. 4.		

Figure 4.1.   **Professional Development Plan—Phase I**

He offers the following suggestions:

- Examine various sources of data on student learning to select a small number of schoolwide, department, or grade-level staff development goals.
- Use faculty, grade-level, and department meetings for learning; minimize time spent on other tasks during these meetings. Use this time for teachers in small groups to review research, consider applications of the findings, and share strategies.
- Find additional opportunities for learning each week by using one or more of the many excellent suggestions for creating time available at www.nsdc.org/library/time.html.
- Focus learning on deepening teachers' knowledge of the content they teach and on expanding the repertoire of instructional strategies available to them so they can successfully teach an increasingly diverse student population.
- Extend training into the classroom by providing extensive coaching and study groups for all teachers. Without intensive follow-up, only a small portion of the learning will make its way into everyday practice in classrooms in a way that improves student learning.
- Organize regularly scheduled meetings for principals focused on the district's learning priorities for students. Teach principals helpful ways to critique one another's school improvement efforts and how to use data and student work in decision making. As with teachers, provide generous amounts of time for small-group discussions.

Follow-up and coaching are imperative for successful implementation and learning.

CHECK FOR UNDERSTANDING

As teachers, we know how essential it is to expect our students to listen, do, practice, and learn from their mistakes. We know how crucial it is to coach them, encourage them, assist them, and check for understanding. How ironic it is that we know and practice what's best for our students' learning yet often fail to demonstrate the same techniques in regard to our own learning.

Certainly, we know the value of checking for understanding. What happens when we fail to check our students for understanding? We run the risk of their not learning or learning incorrectly. We know how difficult it can be to reteach a skill that a student has misunderstood. Checking for understanding and follow-up are keys to students' success.

Helping teachers and administrators learn about data is no different—it's not a one-shot deal. Offering an explanation of definitions and what the data mean is not enough. Most of us don't learn by hearing the information one time. Thus, repeated opportunities for learning will help to ensure understanding.

Let's use as an example data gathered from standardized testing. It is naive to assume that everyone understands such terms as *mean* and *median* or knows the difference between *percentage* and *percentile*. These are terms that can be confusing. Frequent explanations and discussion along with examples of each term are necessary for true understanding. And if we provide opportunities for teachers to hear and use the terms frequently, they are more likely to stick.

Once teachers receive data, follow-up should begin immediately. It is imperative that time be provided for reflecting, reacting, and interacting. Initial follow-up might mean merely providing time to digest and reflect upon the data. Teachers and administrators should be given the opportunity to discuss what they see with each other.

Too often we jump to conclusions about why test results turn out a certain way. We judge and offer excuses or reasons why, before we've had ample time to reflect. Especially if the data appear to be negative, we leap into our defensive mode and offer excuses as to why things look as they do. Ample follow-up opportunities that provide time for reflection, interaction, and discussion will help to foster fair, conscientious analysis.

Perhaps the three most important words when trying to help others understand and learn to use data are *consistent*, *persistent*, and *frequent*. We must be consistent in our message, terminology, and type of data we employ. We must be persistent in our expectations. *Expect* them to use and understand the data appropriately. And make sure that the expecta-

tion of use is frequent—constant. We can't expect teachers to understand and "own" data if they are only expected to look at them once or
twice a year.

MAKE IT ATTRACTIVE, COLORFUL, AND INTERESTING

Even the thought of sitting through a presentation about data makes
some people yawn. Holding their attention can be extremely challeng-
ing. Certainly, making a presentation attractive, colorful, and interesting
will help to hold the attention of the audience. Graphs that are colorful,
bold, and dramatic tend to work best. Caution should be used not to
make a graph too busy or too complicated.

In figure 4.2, data from Southcreek Elementary School is represented
in green, their school color; district data is in blue, the school color of
the district; normed information is in red, white, and blue, representing
a national group of students. Using a simple color coding system helps
the audience more easily identify each group.

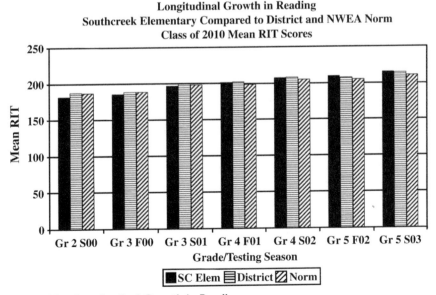

Figure 4.2.   Longitudinal Growth in Reading

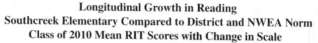

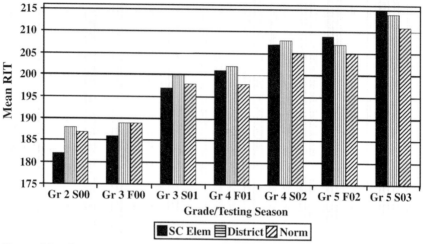

Figure 4.3. Longitudinal Growth in Reading

Changing the scale can make a graph more dramatic. In the two examples below, notice that the data are the same. However, figure 4.3 is much more dramatic than figure 4.2, merely because we have changed the scale. The scale in figure 4.2 is 0–250; the differences are so subtle that they are difficult to distinguish. In figure 4.3 we used a scale of 175–215. The data are the same, but the differences are much more distinctive.

For clarity, we can add data label values. Caution should be used here, again, in order to avoid making the graph too busy and cluttered. Figure 4.4 shows data label values only for the school that is being emphasized.

Adding pictures or icons can emphasize important points you want to make. For example, in figure 4.5 we've used the same graph but have added an explanation of some "good news" in a lighthearted fashion.

Another way to make a presentation more interesting and relevant is to use analogies or stories to convey a concept or emphasize a point. Only by comparing one point of data to another does it derive meaning. In chapter 3, I talked about comparing apples to oranges. Here are a

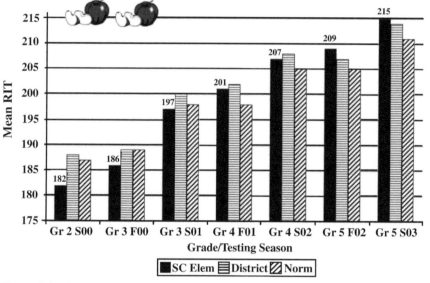

Figure 4.4.   Longitudinal Growth in Reading

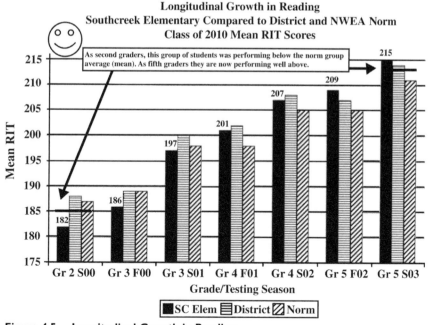

Figure 4.5.   Longitudinal Growth in Reading

couple of examples for explaining the comparison of two different groups of students or two different schools.

Suppose someone were to ask us if we wanted to compare one school to another relative to a state-established spring standard cut off score in reading. At the beginning of the year, the mean score for students in Apple Elementary School is 20 points below the cut score. The mean for Orange Elementary is only 6 points below the cut score. See tables 4.1 and 4.2.

As shown in tables 4.1 and 4.2 and figure 4.6, in the spring, the mean score for Orange Elementary is now 202 or one point above the state cut score. Apple's mean is 196, still five points away from the cut score. Now comes the question of comparison. Can Orange Elementary be considered a better school, since they have "met standard" and Apple Elementary is still five points below the standard?

A colleague of mine, Rick Peters, uses this story about a lion when he is talking about comparative data analogous to this example. It has nothing to do with test scores, but has everything to do with comparing data.

> There were two guys walking through a jungle when a lion appears. One guy asks the other, "Hey! Do you think we can outrun that lion?"
>
> The other guy replies, "I don't care if we can or not. I just want to outrun you! It looks like the lion is the one who's set the target."

The point here is that often data are used to pit one student against another or one school against another. Both schools may be very productive and their students may be making good progress. However, one reaches the target and the other does not. Even though the one that did

Table 4.1. Beginning of the Year Reading Scores Compared to Cut Off Score

	Sept 02
Apple Elementary	181
Orange Elementary	195
State Cut (Spring)	201

Table 4.2. Fall vs. Spring Reading Scores

	Sept 02	May 03
Apple Elementary	181	196
Orange Elementary	195	202
State Cut (Spring)	201	201

not reach the target made significantly more progress toward it than the other, it may still be considered substandard.

My colleague, Parke Smith, tells a story that provides yet another example of the same principle.

Jerry is a new golfer. He bought a new set of clubs and bought the finest in golf attire. He decided to pull his golf bag, rather than renting a cart, so he could get more exercise. Then he went to the golf course and stepped up to the first hole. WHIFF! He missed his first swing. WHIFF! He missed his second swing. He finally made it to the second hole, and the third. It took him three hours and he had a score of 65 for nine holes, not counting the "Mulligans." But Jerry hung in there. By the end of the

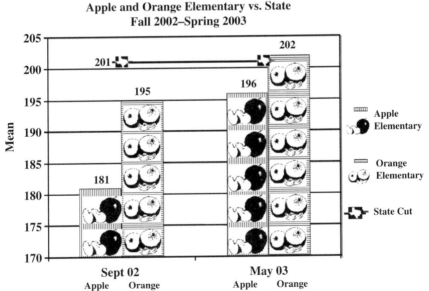

Figure 4.6. Apple and Orange Elementary vs. State, Fall 2002–Spring 2003

season, he was shooting 48 for nine holes, an improvement of 17 strokes. He was "King of the World"—his world.

He decided to go to a real pro course. And who did he run into but Tiger Woods. Now Tiger was finishing a fund raiser for his favorite charity. He had just shot 31 for nine holes and wasn't the least bit excited about his score. Jerry boasted that he had cut 17 strokes off his game this year. He proudly looked at Tiger and said, "What about you? Have you been able to cut 17 strokes off your game?" Tiger just looked at him.

This is another prime example of apples to oranges comparison.

Earlier in this chapter, I mentioned that sometimes definitions that are obvious to those of us who work with data may be confusing to others. Take the terms *percentiles* and *percentages*. A way to explain the difference is to provide pictures or mental models.

A percentage is the score we typically use to grade our students' performance on tests. For example, if we give a student a test with 100 items and the student gets 83 of them correct, we know that the student's percentage is 83. The percentage is a single score based on that one student's performance on the test. A percentage is based on an equal-interval scale.

Percentile, on the other hand, is used when looking at a large group of students to see where they fall in comparison to the others in the group. Think about a mental model of a marathon race. If we were to look at the entire group of racers from overhead, we would see something that looks like figure 4.7.

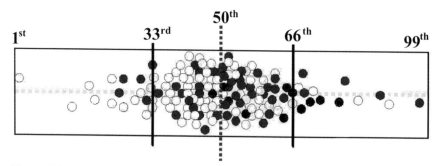

Figure 4.7.   View of Marathon Runners from Overhead

The percentile scale is not an equal-interval scale. From this diagram, we can see that it would be relatively easy for someone to move from the 50th to the 51st percentile. But moving from the seventh percentile to the eighth or ninth would be much more difficult.

Helping our teachers and our public understand concepts such as the ones addressed in this chapter is critical. Being persistent and consistent in our expectations is essential. NWEA executive director Allan Olson advises us that we must use "gentle pressure, relentlessly applied."

5

DON'T SIDESTEP THE ISSUES: DATA CAN BE MISINTERPRETED, BUT IT DOESN'T LIE

I've heard it said that we can make data say anything we want. To some extent, that's true. However, the raw data are extremely useful, and we have an obligation to our students to use data intelligently and responsibly. Educators need not only to learn what data mean, but to help others understand the appropriate use of data.

In *Moments of Truth: New Strategies for Today's Customer-Driven Economy*, Jan Carlzon (1987) states: "An individual without information cannot take responsibility. An individual who is given information cannot help but take responsibility." This is a challenge to educators. We have volumes of data for which we must take responsibility. Our goal should be to learn as much from the data as possible.

LOOK AT DATA IN DIFFERENT WAYS

It is important to look at data in a variety of different ways. As was explained in chapter 3, using a cohort is a means for making an "apples to apples" comparison. Looking at the performance of the same group of students over time is a way to determine their academic growth. Figure 5.1 shows data from a group of students from the spring of

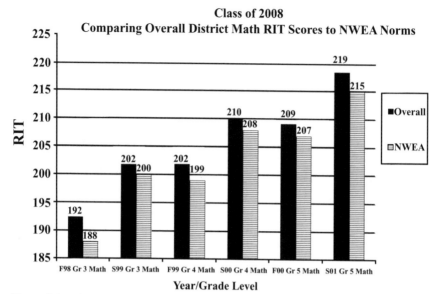

Figure 5.1.   Class of 2008: Comparing Overall District Math RIT Scores to NWEA Norms

their third-grade year to the spring of their fifth-grade year. It shows their overall math RIT scores for each testing season, fall and spring, for each year. It also shows how their scores compare to a norm group. Although it is not as noticeable in this smaller graphic (figure 5.2), the data points on which we want the audience to focus are in a larger font than that of the normed data.

Figure 5.2 adds another data point to the previous graph—performance on the geometry subtest—as it compares to the overall math RIT score. Now, as we emphasize a different piece of the picture, the font size of the goal score is larger and that for the overall math score has been decreased.

LISTEN TO WHAT OTHERS ARE ASKING

Listen to what others are asking, and don't be too quick to jump to the defense. Covey's "seek first to understand, then to be understood" principle was mentioned in chapter 3. It is very wise advice, not only for helping others to understand data but for learning ourselves.

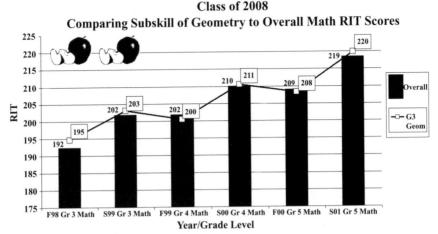

Figure 5.2.   Figure 5.2 Class of 2008: Comparing Subskill of Geometry to Overall Math RIT Scores

A few years back, a mother contacted me to talk about the math programs in our district. She explained that she was aware of two different formats for the same program; one was textbook based, and the other was workbook based. She had been closely monitoring the work of her fourth grader—I'll call Darla—and had tracked her progress. The previous year, Darla's teacher had used the publisher's textbook-based program. This year Darla's fourth-grade teacher was using the workbook program.

Darla's mother believed that the teachers had not had adequate training in this relatively new math program and that Darla was not learning to her potential. She told me that she had spoken with both the teacher and the principal, who had assured her that Darla and the other students were making good progress. Knowing the fine reputation of the principal, I came to the teacher's defense and reinforced what the parent had already been told. She was not totally satisfied but left my office willing to trust that I would look further into the situation.

I pulled out data from the previous year (see figure 5.3) and began to disaggregate the scores. In comparing the fall to spring scores of the teachers using the textbook-based program against the scores of the teachers in the workbook-based program, I discovered a significant difference. There was a four-point difference in the growth of students in the two programs. After digging further, I learned that students in classrooms where the textbook program was being used showed measurably more growth in each of

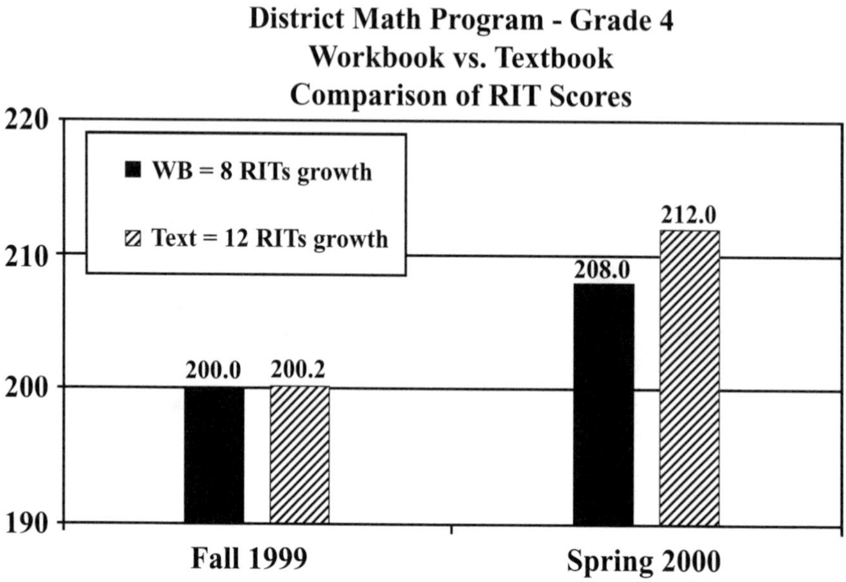

District Math Program - Grade 4
Workbook vs. Textbook
Comparison of RIT Scores

- WB = 8 RITs growth
- Text = 12 RITs growth

Fall 1999: 200.0 200.2
Spring 2000: 208.0 212.0

Fall 1999   **Spring 2000**

Figure 5.3.   District Math Program—Grade 4 Workbook vs. Textbook Comparison
of RIT Scores

the goal areas except for algebra, where the difference was negligible. This
is illustrated in figure 5.4.

We continued to look at other points of data from a couple of other
sources. We also compiled data that allowed us to look at trends over a
couple of years. I thanked Darla's mother for pointing out some things
that caused us to take a close look at our program.

NEVER USE ONLY ONE PIECE OF DATA FOR MAKING DECISIONS

Too often, especially in this age of mandatory statewide testing, the public believes (and many educators, in turn, follow suit) that one source of
data—traditional standardized tests—can be used to solve all of education's perceived ills. "The test" becomes a panacea for improving students' learning. Unfortunately, this mistaken belief has created high-
stakes testing and placed unnecessary pressure on our educators and
students.

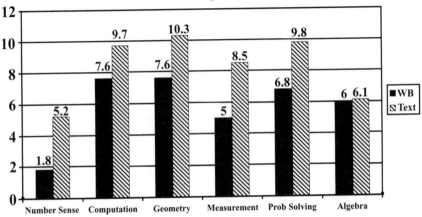

Figure 5.4.   District Math Program—Grade 4 Workbook vs. Textbook Comparison of RIT Growth by Goal Area, Fall 1999–Spring 2000

Numerous sources of data are available to us:

- state test data
- traditional standardized test data
- Northwest Evaluation Association (NWEA) Achievement Level Tests (ALT) or Measures of Academic Progress (MAP)
- teacher observations
- portfolios
- teacher-generated assessments
- attendance records
- commercial worksheets and assessments
- rubrics
- performance tasks
- interest surveys

And the list goes on and on. Sometimes we need to be reminded that data should not be limited to test data. The term *data* is defined by *Webster's New World Dictionary of the American Language* as "things known or assumed; facts from which conclusions can be inferred."

Triangulation is a term used to encourage educators to make decisions based on no fewer than three points of data that generally agree with each other. Two illustrations of an iceberg can help us exemplify the concept of looking at a variety of different sources of data, never relying on just one. These two pictures show the same iceberg from two different angles.

Note that if we focus on one view, we're unable to see some of the points on the iceberg that we can see in the second picture. More importantly, perhaps, is the fact that there are many points we can't see from our perspective above the surface of the water. If we rely on only one point of data in regard to our schools and students, we run the risk of missing other key points for making important decisions. Our children deserve more.

Data are abundant in our schools. We can choose to dance, or we can sit back and watch.

6

TRY SOME FANCY FOOTWORK

Dancing with the data of high-stakes testing can be a frustrating process. Even the most agile and sure-footed professionals experience the perils of tripping, stumbling, and sometimes even falling. The challenges that lie before us as educators are enormous. But I continue to be encouraged by some of the conversations and observations relative to teachers' use and understanding of data. Appropriate use of data to inform instruction is resulting in academic successes of students throughout the country.

We might not all become a Fred Astaire or Ginger Rogers of the data dance world, but we can become successful at using data to better help kids learn. We just need to develop a few strategies for some fancy footwork. Perhaps the COPE strategy is the best place to begin. Let's consider four essential steps based on the following principles:

- Consistency
- Observation
- Persistence
- Education

CONSISTENCY

Find and use sources of consistent data. When making comparisons, make certain that they compare apples to apples, not apples to oranges. Use a common scale in order to make observations about academic growth over time. Compare like groups of students. Always provide students with consistent, appropriate testing environments.

OBSERVATION

Time for observation and reflection is essential before taking any action. Observing the data should always be the first step toward analyzing them. Too often we give in to the temptation of jumping to conclusions about what we think the data tell us. We sometimes blame without taking adequate time to carefully make observations about what we see in the data. Numerous observations and considerations should always precede conclusions. It is often advantageous to utilize the observation talents of many people. One person may see something another might overlook. And don't rely only on the "data geeks." Quite often the less analytical, more creative people lead us to look at things from unique and sometimes revealing perspectives.

PERSISTENCE

People will begin to understand the power of the data only when we are persistent and forthright in our expectations. Merely paying lip service to our expectations is not sufficient. We must lead by example, making data an integral part of the process of change. What we're after is sustained change—change that remains long after the person who initially led the process is gone.

Change can happen in a split second. Sometimes the change is good, sometimes not so good, sometimes undistinguished. Improvement, however, a subset of change, takes time. Sustained improvement only happens when systems change over a period of time—often several years. A simple comparison of the words *change* and *improvement* can lead us to some profound insight. *Change* is a six-letter word, and change can happen very quickly. *Improvement*, on the other hand, is a word five letters longer, and improvement takes time. Think of the five additional letters as five years. In order for sustained change to happen, build upon a five-year plan.

John P. Kotter, in *Leading Change*, identifies eight errors common to organizational change efforts:

1. Allowing too much complacency.
2. Failing to create a sufficiently powerful guiding coalition.
3. Underestimating the power of vision.
4. Undercommunicating the vision by a factor of 10 (or even 100 or even 1,000).
5. Permitting obstacles to block the new vision.
6. Failing to create short-term wins.
7. Declaring victory too soon.
8. Neglecting to anchor changes firmly in the corporate culture.

Each of these represents a period of time that should be built into the change process. Persistence over a short time span of a few weeks is relatively easy compared to being persistent through a period of several years.

Leading a group of people to make sustained improvements can only happen if a level of trust and commitment exists within the group. While relationship building may not appear to be directly related to data initially, it is a vital component. Getting the partners together is an obvious first step essential to making the dance happen.

To assist in developing trust and relationships within the school organization, I recommend *Living on a Tightrope: A Survival Handbook for Principals* by Ruby K. Payne and William A. Sommers (2002). This book provides insight into balancing the component tasks of educational management: managing relationships, managing power, and managing identity.

EDUCATION

Ironic as it is, although we are educators, we sometimes ignore the education of others to understand and appropriately use data. We teach teachers how to administer a test, how to teach kids to take a test, and too often how to teach *to* the test. Every year we provide administrators, parents, and the media with mountains of data, yet we often fail miserably in helping them understand how to use the data appropriately. Somehow we seem to think that "they should just know."

The single most important step in this dance with data is education. It is so obvious, yet so often ignored. The key to successful, sustained change in process is educating others in the need for change, the process, and the basic principles of the components of the change process. Finding and taking the time to learn and teach others about how to dance with the data will result in huge dividends for our children.

GLOSSARY

actual anticipated normal curve equivalent (AANCE) An expected or anticipated score based on the child's intellectual ability, typically derived from a test of cognitive skills.

assessment The use of various methods to obtain information about student learning that can be used to guide a variety of decisions and actions.

cognitive skills index (CSI) An age-based score that describes the child's performance on an aptitude test. A score of 100 is considered average.

constructed-response item A test question/item that requires the test-taker to create his or her own response (for example, a short-answer, essay, pictorial, or graphic response).

criterion-referenced tests An approach for describing a student's performance according to established criteria. The focus is on performance of an individual as measured against a standard or criteria rather than against performance of others who take the same test, as with norm-referenced tests. Criterion-referenced test scores report a student's performance on predefined educational objectives. Scores from these tests indicate the degree to which a student has mastered a content or skill area.

curriculum alignment   The process of linking content and performance standards to assessment, instruction, and learning in classrooms.

ISTEP+   Indiana Statewide Testing for Educational Progress. This is a criterion-referenced standardized test for assessing students relative to the Indiana Academic Standards. Most states assess students using similar statewide tests.

mean anticipated normal curve equivalent (MANCE)   The mean or average expected or anticipated score of a group of students based on their ability derived from the CSI scores.

mean normal curve equivalent (MNCE)   The actual average (mean) normal curve equivalent (NCE) of a group of students.

mixed format test   A test that uses different types of test items, which may include multiple-choice, short-answer, essay questions, and performance tasks.

multiple-choice item   A test item, question, or incomplete statement that is followed by a set of possible answer choices, one of which is the correct answer. Multiple-choice items may also be referred to as "selected-response" items.

national percentile (NP)   The student's performance is compared to a predetermined, nationally selected group of students whose characteristics are known. The percentile indicates the percentage of students in the norm group whose scores fall below a particular student's score. An NP of 71 means that the student scored as well as or higher than 71 percent of the students in the norm group.

normal curve equivalent (NCE)   A measure like percentiles, except that the scale is divided into 99 equal-interval scales. This means that NCE scores from different tests can be compared. These types of comparisons cannot be made using national percentiles (NP). If a student receives NCE scores of 53 on the reading test and 45 on the math test, it is correct to say that the reading score is eight points higher than the math score.

norm-referenced test scores   Norm-referenced test scores compare the student's performance to that of students in a norm or "typical group" of students, generally nationwide. They show where students stand in relation to their peers, rather than to a defined standard of achievement.

open-ended item   A question or problem designed to require students to apply their knowledge or understanding of a concept.

performance assessment   An evaluation in which students are asked to engage in a complex task, often involving the creation of a product. Student performance is rated based on the process the student engages in or the product of the task.

rubric   A defined criterion for appraising a student's individual work. A rubric typically outlines specific levels or degrees of completion or expectation, often on a four- or five-point scale.

standardized achievement test   Typically, commercially designed tests for which content has been selected and standardized so that administration and scoring procedures are the same for all test-takers.

BIBLIOGRAPHY

Airasian, P. W., & Madaus, G. F. (1983). Linking testing and instruction: Policy issues. *Journal of Educational Measurement* 20 (2): 103–18.

Baker, E. L. (1989). Can we fairly measure the quality of education? (CSE Tech. Rep. No. 290 Grant No. OERI-G-86-0003). Los Angeles: University of California Center for Research on Evaluation, Standards, and Student Testing.

Bernhardt, V. L. (1998). *Data analysis for comprehensive schoolwide improvement*. Larchmont, NY: Eye on Education, Inc.

Bernhardt, V. L. (1999). *The school portfolio*. Larchmont, NY: Eye on Education, Inc.

Bernhardt, V. L. (2000). *Designing and using databases for school improvement*. Larchmont, NY: Eye on Education, Inc.

Bond, L. A. (1997). Trends in state student assessment programs, Fall 1996. Washington, DC: Council of Chief Sate School Officers, U.S. Department of Education, Office of Educational Research and Improvement, Educational Resources Information Center.

Bond, L. A., Braskamp, D., & Roeber, E. D. (1996). *The status of state student assessment programs in the United States*. Oak Brook, IL: North Central Regional Educational Laboratory and Council of Chief State School Officers.

Bowers, B. C. (1989). Alternatives to standardized educational assessment. ERIC Digest. EA 40, EA 312773, EA 021431.

Cannell, J. J. (1987). Nationally normed elementary achievement testing in America's public schools: How all 50 states are above the national average. *Educational Measurement: Issues and Practice* 7 (4): 12–15.

Carlzon, J. (1987). *Moments of truth: New strategies for today's customer-driven economy*. Cambridge, MA: Ballinger Publishing.

dePaolo, R. (1993, March). A nation at risk—still. *Across the board*.

Dietel, R. J., Herman, J. L., & Knuth, R. A. (1991). What does research say about assessment? Oak Brook, IL: North Central Regional Educational Laboratory.

Doyle, W. (1983). Academic work. *Review of Educational Research* 53 (2): 159–99.

Ebel, R. L. (1972). *Essentials of educational measurement*. Englewood Cliffs, NJ: Prentice Hall.

Franklin Community School Corporation. (1997). ISTEP+ survey. Franklin, Indiana.

Fredericksen, N. (1984). The real test bias: Influences of testing of teaching and learning. *American Psychologist* 39 (3): 193–202.

Freeman, D. J., Kuhs, T. M, Porter, A. C., Floden, R. E., Schmidt, W. H., & Schwille, J. R. (1983). Do textbooks and tests define a natural curriculum in elementary school mathematics? *Elementary School Journal* 83 (5): 501–13.

Gardner, E. (1982, December). Five common misuses of tests. ERIC Digest no. 108.

Gilman, D., & Andrew, R. (1996). What are some difficulties with statewide performance assessment? *Bulletin*, December 1996, 67–75.

Gilman, D. A. & Reynolds, L. L. (1991). The side effects of state-wide testing. *Contemporary Education* 62 (4): 273–78.

Glaser, R., & Silver, E. (1994). Assessment, testing, and instruction: Retrospect and prospect. Los Angeles: National Center for Research on Evaluation, Standards, and Student Testing.

Gleason, B. (2000). National survey gauges parent perceptions of state-mandated, standardized tests. Alexandria, VA: Association for Supervision and Curriculum Development.

Green, K. E., & Stager, S. E. (1986). Measuring attitudes of teachers towards testing. *Measurements and Evaluation in Counseling and Development* 9: 141–50.

Gucwa, B., & Mastie, M. (1989). *Pencils down: A guide for using and reporting test results*. Lansing, MI: Michigan State Board of Education.

Haertel, E. (1989). Student achievement tests as tools of educational policy: Practices and consequences. In B. R. Gifford (ed.), *Test policy and test performance: Education, language and culture*. Boston: Kluwer Academic Publishers.

Haladyna, T., Nolen, S. B., & Haas, N. S. (1991). Raising standardized achievement test scores and the origins of test score pollution. *Educational Researcher* 20 (5): 2–7.

Herman, J. L. (1989). Priorities of educational testing and evaluation: The testimony of the CRESST national faculty (CSE Tech. Rep. No. 304). Los Angeles: University of California, Center for the Study of Evaluation.

Herman, J. L. (1994). Assessing the effects of standardized testing on schools. *Educational and psychological measurement* 54 (2): 471–82.

Herman, J. L., Dreyfus, J., & Golan, S. (1990). The effects of testing on teaching and learning (CSE Tech. Rep. No. 327, Grant No. OERI-G-86-0003). Los Angeles: University of California, Center for Research on Evaluation, Standards, and Student Testing.

Hopfenberg, W. S., Levin, H., Meister, G., & Roers, J. (1990). Accelerated schools. Accelerated schools project paper, Stanford University, Stanford, CA.

Fullen, M. G., with Stieglbauer, S. (1991). *The new meaning of educational change.* New York: Teachers College Press.

Indiana Department of Education. (1990). *Indiana statewide testing for educational progress (ISTEP), initial assessment and general report 1987–1989.*

Indiana Department of Education. (1998, Fall). *Guide to test interpretation.* Monterey, CA: CTB/McGraw-Hill.

Jones, C. J. (1998). *Curriculum-based assessment: The easy way.* Springfield, IL: Charles C. Thomas.

Joyce, B., Wolf, J., & Calhoun, E. (1993). *The self-renewing school.* Alexandria, VA: Association for Supervision and Curriculum Development.

Kandel, I. L. (1936). *Examinations and their substitutes in the United States.* Bulletin No. 28. New York: Carnegie Foundation for the Advancement of Teaching.

Kirst, M. W. (1979). The new politics of state education finance. *Phi Delta Kappan* 60 (6): 425–32.

Kotter, J. P. (1996). *Leading change.* Cambridge, MA: Harvard Business School Press.

Lemann, N. (1999). *The big test: The secret history of the American meritocracy.* New York: Farrar, Straus, & Giroux.

Linden, J. D., & Linden, K. W. (1968). *Tests on trial.* Boston: Houghton Mifflin.

Linn, R. L., Graue, M. E., & Sanders, N. M. (1989). Comparing state and district test results to national norms: Interpretations of scoring "above the national average" (Technical Report, Grant No. ERI-G-86-0063). Boulder: University of Colorado, Center for Research on Evaluation, Standards, and Student Testing.

Lyman, H. B. (1997). *Test scores and what they mean.* Needham Heights, MA: Allyn & Bacon.

Marzano, R. J., Pickering, D., & McTighe, J. (1994). *Assessing student outcomes: Performance assessment using the dimensions of learning model.* Arlington, VA: Association for Vision and Curriculum Development.

McCleery, B. (2001, January 19). Educators say comparing schools can be misleading. *Indianapolis Star*.

McDonnell, L. M., McLaughlin, M. J., & Morison, P., eds. (1997). *Educating one and all: Students with disabilities and standards-based reform*. Washington, DC: National Academy Press.

Morison, R. (1992). Testing in American schools: Issues for research and policy. *Social Policy Report* 6 (2): 1–24.

National Commission on Excellence in Education. (1983). *A Nation at risk: The imperative for educational reform*. Washington, DC: U.S. Department of Education.

National Research Council. (1989). *Annual report of the Mathematical Sciences Education Board*.

Nolen, S. B., Haladyna, T. M., & Hass, N. S. (1989). A survey of Arizona teachers and school administrators on the uses and effects of standardized achievement testing (Tech. Rep. No 89-2). Phoenix: Arizona State University, West Campus.

Nolen, S. B., Haladyna, T. M., & Haas, N. S. (1992). Uses and abuses of achievement test scores. *Educational Measurement: Issues and Practice* 11 (2): 9–15.

Noll, V. H., & Scannel, D. P. (1972). *Introduction to educational measurement*, 3rd ed. Boston: Houghton Mifflin.

Northwest Evaluation Association (NWEA), 5585 SW Meadows Rd., Suite 200, Lake Oswego, OR, www.nwea.org.

Payne, R. K., & Magee, D. S. (1999). *Meeting standards and raising test scores when you don't have much time or money*. Highlands, TX: RFT Publishing.

Payne, R. K., & Sommers, W. A. (2000). *Living on a tightrope: A survival handbook for principals*. Highlands, TX: Aha! Process, Inc.

Peterson, J. J. (1983). *The Iowa testing programs: The first 50 years*. Iowa City: University of Iowa Press.

Popham, W. J. (1999). Why standardized tests don't measure educational quality. *Educational Leadership* 56 (6).

Resnick, L. B., & Resnick, D. P. (1992). Assessing the thinking curriculum: New tools for educational reform. In B. R. Gifford & M. C. O'Connor, eds., *Changing assessments: Alternative views of aptitude, achievement, and instruction*. Boston: Kluwer Academic Publishers.

Robinson, G. E., & Craver, J. M. (1989). *Assessing and grading student achievement*. Arlington, VA: Educational Research Service.

Roeber, E. D. (1995). Critical issue: Reporting assessment results. Oak Brook, IL: North Central Regional Educational Laboratory.

Rombert, T. A., Zarinnia, A., & Williams, S. R. (1989). *The influence of mandated testing on mathematics instruction: Grade 8 teachers' perceptions*.

Madison: University of Wisconsin, National Center for Research in Mathematical Sciences Education.

Rosenholtz, S. J. (1991). *Teacher's workplace: The social organization of schools*. New York: Teachers College Press.

Sanders, W. L., & Horn, S. P. (1995). The usefulness of standardized and alternative measures of student achievement as indicators for the assessment of educational outcomes. *Educational Policy Analysis Archives* 3 (6): 1–12.

Schmoker, M. (1996). *Results: The key to continuous school improvement*. Alexandria, VA: Association for Supervision and Curriculum Development.

Schmoker, M. (1997). Occupational knowledge and the inevitability of school improvement. *Phi Delta Kappan* 78 (7): 560–63.

Shepard, L. A. (1990). Inflated test score gains: Is it old norms or teaching the test? *Educational Measurement: Issues and Practices* 9 (3): 15–22.

Shepard, L. A. (1995). Using assessments to improve learning. *Educational Leadership*, 52 (5): 38.

Smith, M. L. (1991a). Meanings of test preparation. *American Educational Research Journal* 28 (3): 521–42.

Smith, M. L. (1991b). Put to the test: The effects of external testing on teachers. *Educational Researcher* 20 (5): 8–11.

Smith, M. L., Edelsky, C., Draper, K., Rottenberg, C., & Chyerland, M. (1989). *The role of testing in elementary schools* (Monograph, Grant No. OERI-G-86-003). Tempe: Arizona State University, Center for Research on Evaluation, Standards, and Student Testing.

Solomon, P. G. (1998). *The curriculum bridge: From standards to actual classroom practice*. Thousand Oaks, CA: Corwin Press.

Sparks, D. (2000, September). Six ways to immediately improve professional development. *Results* newsletter. National Staff Development Council, www.nsdc.org.

Thomas, K., & DeBarros, A. (2002, August 5). 19 of USA's "finest" schools are "failing." *USA Today* 1A.

Urdan, T. (1994). Teachers' perceptions of standardized achievement tests. *Educational Policy* 8 (2): 137–57.

Wiggins, G. (1989a). A true test: Toward more authentic and equitable assessment. *Phi Delta Kappan* 70 (9): 703–13.

Wiggins, G. (1989b). Teaching to the (authentic) test. *Educational Leadership* 46 (7): 41–47.

Wiggins, G. (1994). None of the above. *Executive Educator* 16 (7): 14–18.

ABOUT THE AUTHOR

Dave Sever was born in Shelbyville, Indiana, on June 11, 1951. Raised in Waldron, Indiana, he attended Waldron School and graduated from Waldron High School in 1969. He received a bachelor of science from Ball State University in 1972, a master of science from Indiana University in 1975, and a specialist in education degree from Indiana University in 1984, and he completed school superintendent certification requirements in 1989 at Indiana University. In 1999, he earned a Ph.D. in education leadership from Indiana State University.

He began his career in education as an elementary teacher at Triton Elementary School in the Northwestern Consolidated School Corporation of Shelby County in 1972. Following seven years of teaching in grades 4, 5, and 6, he served as acting principal at Triton Elementary, then as principal from 1978 until 1987. From 1987 until 1990 he was principal of Union Elementary School with the Franklin Community School Corporation in Franklin, Indiana. After serving as director of elementary education and curriculum from 1990 until 1994, he became director of K–12 curriculum. In 1998 he was named assistant superintendent. He has served in numerous leadership capacities, including president of the Triton Classroom Teachers Association, president of the Johnson County Community Network, and president

of the Johnson County Step Ahead Council. In 1994 he was appointed
by Governor Evan Bayh to the Indiana Step Ahead Panel, and he was
a chief founder of Franklin's Community Involvement in Learning organization.

Sever has presented at numerous state and national conferences on
topics such as assessment, technology, and community involvement. He
is currently client development coordinator for Northwest Evaluation
Association.